Parent POWER

Godly Influence in an Age of Weakness

■ David R. Miller ■

ACCENT BOOKS
Denver, Colorado

All names and case studies in this book are based on true experiences, but they have been altered to respect the privacy of the individuals involved.

All Scripture taken from King James Version of the Bible.

A division of Accent Publications, Inc.
12100 West Sixth Avenue
P.O. Box 15337
Denver, Colorado 80215

Library of Congress Catalog Card Number 87-73391

ISBN 0-89636-245-0

Cover by J. William Coburn

To Linda
the perfect wife

CONTENTS

Contents

FOREWORD

The traditional American family is under siege as never before. Forces tearing at the fabric of life are relentless in their attacks on the sanctity of marriage, the two-parent family unit, and the moral roots that give our children the stability to withstand the winds of change.

Parenting is the battleground, the weak spot so often exploited by those who would see other institutions replace the family as the transmitter of culture and godly knowledge to our children. We parents are being bombarded with the messages of hedonism telling us to do what feels good for *us* and to quit worrying about how the children will react. "Do your own thing" is the death knell of increasing numbers of families, sadly, even within the Christian community.

But Christian families have an answer to this weakness, and that answer is found in learning what God would have us know about the use of parent power in the Christian family. In an age of geopolitics and constant rumors of war, power has come to have a negative meaning in many minds. But power under the guidance of the Holy Spirit and within the framework of an inerrant Bible is a tool God expects Christian parents to use.

Dr. David Miller, writer, teacher, counselor, and parent, explores the element of power missing in many Christian families struggling to raise children. As parents represent God to the mind of a young child, so parents must express that unique brand of loving authority God exercises in our lives as Christians. Developing child-rearing practices within Biblical teaching must include an appreciation for that godly influence, that power parents have under God to guide and direct their children.

Dr. Miller is not afraid to tackle the difficult areas of Christian parenting. He writes from practical experience as a parent and as a family counselor. His insights and comments can become one of God's instruments to help strengthen Christian families. This book should become a valuable part of your training as you face the frustrations and obstacles created by this increasingly sin-ridden world. God bless you in your service to Him as a parent.

Jerry Falwell
Lynchburg, Virginia

INTRODUCTION

Joshua saw his people wavering in their commitment to the Lord, and like many prophets of his day, exhorted them to choose the true God or fall into idol worship. Joshua didn't bargain, plead, or promise. Joshua didn't compromise. Joshua confronted the people with a choice.

"And if it seem evil unto you to serve the Lord, choose you this day whom ye will serve."   Joshua 24:15a

And then Joshua stood up before the people, his family in a sense, and proclaimed,

". . . but for me and my house, we will serve the Lord."

Joshua was speaking for *his* family, his "house," when he made this bold commitment, one that contained no emergency retreat plans.

Joshua didn't proclaim, ". . . but for me and my house, we *might* serve the Lord." He didn't promise God to "try" to serve Him or to give it his best effort. Joshua said *we will* serve the Lord.

". . . but for me and my house, we will *serve the Lord."*

Consider the power in that statement, the sense of certainty that God would provide the means to do the right thing. Think of the "no retreat, no compromise" implicit in this prophet's commitment to God.

And Joshua didn't stop with making his own commitment to God. He included his family, *all* of his family in the promise.

A secular person looking at this would probably think that Joshua was either insane—or knew something no one else knew.

What gave Joshua that sense of power? What gave him the confidence to say what *would* happen instead of what *might*

9

happen? What enabled Joshua to do what so many parents have trouble doing today, making a firm commitment to God on behalf of their family, their "house"?

Joshua knew from experience that God was all powerful, a loving and compassionate God who would not tolerate sin and unholiness. He had seen what we can only read about, and his mind was not confused with the present attempts at corrupting the family unit. Joshua battled the Amorites, but he did not battle his own family. Joshua was God's man in his nation *and* in his family. He was as willing to trust God for wisdom and direction in the smaller aspects of family life as he was in being God's voice in the land.

Joshua was powerful because he trusted God and *acted* like it!

Perfection in Parenting

Perfection is an unreasonable goal for Christian parents. Being as powerful and influential with our children as we would like to be is an often hoped for but seldom realized goal. But in this sin-ridden world, being the best parents we can be, under the circumstances God places us in, is being perfect in God's eyes. God never asks more of us than we are able to bear, even when it comes to raising our children.

Maybe being good parents, the best *we* can be under God and within His rules for living, maybe this is as close as we can get to perfection in this life. Discovering this truth should relieve a lot of Christian parents. God does not expect perfection from us in any other area of life. Why should we think He expects us to be perfect parents?

In Search of Good Christian Parents

Perhaps we could ask parents whose children became missionaries, successful business people, doctors, engineers, or preachers of the gospel, what they did to get such great results from their efforts. We could talk to folks whose grown children have not divorced, who are not addicted to anything, and have never been even suspected of a crime. Surely the

10

final product, mature adult children, is a fair way to evaluate the quality of Christian parenting.

Unfortunately, it's not.

Think of all the people who overcame difficult family situations to become terrific Christian people. We all know some who had alcoholic parents, others who had mental illness in the home, and others who were abused in the worst ways possible. But they made it. God carried them through the valley of the shadow of bad parenting and they turned out great.

We know still others from seemingly perfect homes who grew up to be morally bankrupt, an affront to God and all who know Him. We see children who grew up to confuse and disappoint their good parents, seemingly intent on destroying everything their parents held dear.

The fact of the matter is, that while the quality of home life and the spiritual values of parents are very important in growing good children, nothing we do as parents can contradict the principle of free will found in the Bible. (II Timothy 1:8-9; Romans 14:11-12). God has no grand-children. Each child, adolescent, or adult chooses his direction for life either within or without the will of God.

Influenced by good or bad parenting? Yes!

Controlled? No!

Judging Self or Others

Understanding the role of power in Christian parenting depends in large measure on our ability to suspend judgment of self and others. This is a difficult task because we are so accustomed to grading and evaluating everything from kindergarten on up. But judgment is one of the main reasons parents lose power with their younger children and teenagers. Control of the judgment reflex is worth some effort.

Several years ago our family was in attendance at the Sunday evening service of the Hampton Park Baptist Church in Greenville, South Carolina. Actually, I had our three

11

children with me because Linda had to answer a hospital call and go to work.

So it was just Dad and the kids at church. The children were 6, 10, and 13 at the time, and we were enjoying the relaxed atmosphere. At the conclusion of the service, an older man seated behind us leaned over, shook my hand, and complimented me on how well-behaved my children were during church.

Thank God for compliments, but I knew that our kids had been raised to show respect for God's house and were under threat of death, dismemberment, or worse for acting up in church.

They *had* to behave!

There was no choice involved. I accepted the kind compliment, but I also knew that it took no particular skill on my part to have well-behaved children in church. I simply had to decide to have obedience and respect in church, be willing to enforce that decision, and it was done.

It was my *will,* not my skill as a parent that produced good behavior in our young children.

But there are times when we all feel like evaluating the performance of others. We have all seen the tantruming child in the supermarket who screams and cries and wants his way no matter what—and usually gets it!

We think to ourselves, "Why doesn't she take that kid outside and spank him?" Usually we conclude that the mother is a bad parent for giving in to the tantrum.

Or how about the teenager who misbehaves in church, whispering and passing notes, scribbling in the hymnal, his parents sitting right there! Don't they notice what's going on? How can they sit there with that blissful smile on their faces and listen to the message without controlling their teen-ager?

The point is that any parent who wills it can control small children. Teenagers are hard to control by even the very best parents. Young adults are not going to be controlled by their parents in any case.

Your parent power is determined by your will, not your skill. Skill in parenting is important, but will is indispensable. Power in parenting is impossible without a conscious choice on the part of Christian parents to control, influence, and change the behavior of their children and teenagers.

This book in your hands is meant to encourage parents to be *powerful* parents.

I hope *you* find this book useful.

1
POWER-FULL PARENTING

Jeff was out of control! He had been suspended from his junior high school twice in one semester for fighting and being disrespectful to teachers. His parents were sure he was getting involved with drugs and alcohol although they couldn't prove it yet. Jeff was staying out later and later and had not even come home at all a few nights. Worst of all, he had recently hit his mother when she challenged him about who his companions would be.

For a fourteen-year-old from a solid Christian family, Jeff was heading fast for the deep-end, and his parents were in a panic over what to do about it.

Jeff's parents felt powerless, and they were right!

When Angelo came in to see me, he didn't look like the tyrant his mother made him out to be. I soon discovered that looks can be deceiving!

Angelo was in my office at his mother's insistence because he had recently begun spending about three nights a week with his nineteen-year-old girlfriend in her apartment.

Angelo was only sixteen, the oldest son of divorced parents. Angelo's mother and older sister had been saved about two years before, and while he was not against religion, Angelo did not feel that his mother had any business telling him what to do with his time. His mother felt guilty about the divorce and the fact that her ex-husband did not want to see the children any more. She was reluctant to confront her son about his behavior. At the time we talked, Angelo lived at home most of the time, and his mother still did all his laundry, cleaned and cooked for him, and paid his car insurance.

15

Angelo's mom felt powerless, too!

When Pastor Bowles called about Susan Wilson, I already knew from our high schoolers what had happened. Susan was expelled for telling lies about supposed drug use, writing notes about her "drug experiences" to other kids, and then lying about it when confronted.

Susan was a ninth grader at the time; her father was the business manager for the church and school; her mother taught fourth grade in the elementary school.

As I talked with the pastor, it became clear that one of the major problems was the family's embarrassment about Susan's behavior. Mom and Dad were talking about putting Susan in one of the Christian boarding schools for difficult teenage girls in Texas. I agreed with Pastor Bowles that this seemed an extreme measure for the kind of offense committed, but the parents had just about made up their minds.

As I talked with the family, it was clear that the decision to have Susan live somewhere else was about 99% sure. A few days later, Susan and her mom flew to Texas.

They were powerless, too, but for different reasons.

Parent Power

Each set of parents in these real-life examples had the same problem—lack of power. Each had started out with the same amount of power, 100%, and each had lost, given away, or surrendered their power to others. The power loss so evident in these three families would change the lives of the children involved for the worse. The saddest thing of all is that these parents did not have to lose their power with their children. They could have remained almost as strong and influential as they were when the child was small if they had just been more aware of the slow erosion of the power God gave them when He allowed them to become parents.

We will look at some specifics of power loss in the next chapter. For now, let's concentrate on these three families, what happened to produce their power loss, and how each worked to try to get their power back.

Remember that just as God intended children to have two parents, He also intended that those parents remain forces for good in the lives of their children. Power is as basic to good parenting as providing food and shelter—and in some ways is more important.

Jeff

What brought Jeff to the point of striking his mother?

This is such a deviant form of child and adolescent behavior that I totally agreed with Jeff's parents about the need to do something.

Jeff was only fourteen and had been a problem for only a year. But what a year! He was in trouble with everybody. He was forbidden to be in the homes of some of his friends; he had a police record for breaking and entering an empty house; he had run away twice, and had admitted to drug and alcohol experimentation.

This is a kid from a Christian family who is just fourteen!

After several counseling sessions with his parents, I saw Jeff for the first time.

I have never seen a child who so clearly presented an impression of rebellion. It was all over him. He sulked, refusing to talk unless it was negative comments about his parents. He wouldn't look at me eye-to-eye, and he did not conceal his unwillingness to be there in my office. He had bleached his hair in stripes and was dressed to appear as rebellious as possible.

After much careful counseling, it became clear to me that what had happened to Jeff was a direct result of the loss of power by his father. This was not an easy conclusion to reach. It took several weeks of counseling with his parents and Jeff, but it was unavoidable.

At one point I asked Jeff's dad how he felt about the specific incident of Jeff hitting his mother. After a long and very emotional pause, he answered that it so bothered him that he was almost out of control about it.

I asked if anything like this had ever happened in his family as he was growing up. He replied that nothing even

17

close had ever happened.

When I asked him what *his* father would have done if *he* had ever hit his mother, his response was quick and definite.

"He would have killed me!"

"Mr. Collins, why hasn't Jeff seen that kind of fatherly power in you?"

Silence

Then tears.

We went on to talk about what the absence of power does to children and how we, sometimes, are reluctant to use our power because we have bought the world's lie that power must always be bad for children. Exactly the opposite was happening here. Jeff was being destroyed by the void created when his father refused to exercise his authority. If Jeff was to be rescued from the potential lifestyle he had set for himself, Dad was going to have to re-assert that God-given power.

But how to do it?

Patterns of parenting are hard to change, but when there is a strong commitment by parents, and a lot of prayer, it can be done. We developed a series of steps to be implemented with Jeff. They began with family counseling sessions where I would set up a plan for the parents to follow when Jeff misbehaved the next time.

Mr. and Mrs. Collins agreed that if Jeff would not correct his behavior, an alternate living environment might be necessary. This was an important step for them. Heretofore, they had resisted the idea of long-term danger to Jeff and only now decided that the end of their rope was fast approaching.

Together we decided that Jeff would lose a variety of privileges for school problems beginning with confiscation of his beloved skateboard for three days for every one day of school suspension in the future. If he ran away overnight again, his room would be stripped bare of everything but his bed for one month. If he missed curfew, he would lose both his skateboard and his bike for a week. And if he ever hit his mother again, his father would deal with him man to man, and after they picked up the pieces, they would find a

18

boarding home for him for the rest of the school year or longer.

For the first time I could see Mr. Collins walking a little taller as they left the office, and Mrs. Collins was smiling for the first time in a long time.

Mr. Collins was becoming *a father* again, and it must have felt very good!

How did it turn out?

Well, as we expected, Jeff challenged the new system, but after a few months of experiencing all the measures we discussed, he is starting to come around.

We cannot kid ourselves. Several years of bad parenting will not be fixed overnight. We can only start with the first step.

I still see Jeff on a weekly basis, and he has a ways to go yet. But the changes I see in him reflect his grudging agreement that Mom and Dad *are* in charge again.

The changes in Jeff are a result of Mr. Collins's realization that God does not want parents to be weak, and if he is to be an obedient Christian parent, he *must* exercise his God-given parent power. Now Jeff has a chance!

Angelo

Experts tell us that by 1991, between 40% and 50% of children under 18 will have spent at least part of their childhood years living with just one parent. Using today's statistics, we know that *most* children with divorced parents have not seen the absent parent at all during the last calendar year. Ninety-two percent of the time, the absent parent is the father.

Angelo and his mom are included in those statistics, and they cost Mrs. Daversa her parent power.

Angelo was as out-of-control as Jeff in the beginning, and for the same general reasons. Angelo's mother never really recovered from the rejection of her divorce. It takes two to make a marriage, but only one to make a divorce. Mrs. Daversa did not want the divorce, and believed she had failed both her marriage and her children when it happened.

She lost her parent power to guilt. Mrs. Daversa was so

consumed with self-blame and doubt about her own worth that she did not have the strength of will to challenge her son on his behavior. Her problems with Angelo were a direct result of not understanding that God's power is not dependent on circumstances in the parent's life. Angelo should not have been allowed to become his own parent, but his mother was too busy trying to *earn* his love because she felt like a bad parent.

This self-fulfilling prophecy is not unusual in families suffering a divorce. Parents in this situation often feel the need to live life as an apology to their children, constantly trying to make up for their children growing up with only one parent—even though the individual parent may not have wanted the divorce.

Mrs. Daversa has a long way to go to restore the power she needs right now. We pray a lot in our counseling sessions because we know there is not much time for Angelo. A few more years, and he will be on his own. There will not be the need or the opportunity for the parent power that is so important now.

Counseling with Angelo has not been very successful so far. He is so angry at his father for leaving him, and so angry at his mother for causing, as he believes, the divorce, that he is not willing to sit still and listen to what God is trying to say to him through his problems. The outlook for Angelo is not good unless a miracle of regeneration takes place. Right now, he wants nothing to do with a God he believes gave him a bad deal in life.

We are still working with Mrs. Daversa and Angelo.

Susan

Susan's parents are good Christian parents in everyone's eyes but theirs. Because they are so involved in the work of a large church and school, the misbehavior of their daughter is an extra heavy blow to their family. They *felt* like pretty good Christian parents until Susan started having her problems. Because Susan is the oldest child and the first teenager, her parents tended to do what most Christian parents do with their oldest child—overreact!

20

Susan needed counseling to determine her reasons for making up the stories that got her into so much trouble. She needed a listening ear, one that would not judge or criticize, one that would listen.

But her parents' sense of shame and embarrassment made it impossible for them to keep her at home while working on the problem. Mr. and Mrs. Wilson felt the need to let other parents know that *they* were not going to sit idly by and let Susan get away with aberrant behavior.

Susan's parents had lost nearly all their parent power to their legalistic attitudes and their embarrassment over her behavior. We have to look like good parents, they thought, and we must *do* something even if it means having our daughter live elsewhere for awhile. It was simply impossible for Mr. and Mrs. Wilson to cut through their own need for respectability and put the well-being of their daughter ahead of their own needs.

Susan's parents have assigned control of her life to someone else for a time, and they will never get their parent power back with her. They have told Susan through their actions that they could not handle her problems, but Susan will know for the rest of her life that they *would* not handle her problems.

Susan will come home next year. Maybe sooner. But things will not be the same for Susan and her parents. She will have learned by then that love and power in families are inseparable. She will have learned also that her parents' willingness to sacrifice their power to help her means that they love themselves and their reputation more than they love Susan.

Susan *and* her parents will have realized a very sad lesson about parent power, a lesson that will be with Susan all her life. It is a lesson I hope readers of this book never have to learn.

The Power of Holy Spirit Parenting

The Bible tells us that God is a God of power (Psalm 62:11; Matthew 19:26). The Creator of the universe, the Alpha and

21

Omega, God is the source of all power.

God has provided parents with a Comforter, the Holy Spirit, to walk along beside us and share our burdens for our children. The work of the Holy Spirit leads us in making those decisions about our children that are not clearly spelled out in Scripture. When we are asked to make a decision about attendance at a movie, a date for a teenager, or how to discipline an uncommon child, we are to rely on the Holy Spirit for guidance. As we rely upon prayer and the Bible, we will know our decisions are sound because the Holy Spirit cannot encourage us to do something that is contradicted in the Bible.

But *we* are to make the decision under God.

We are *not* to place the opinion of "experts" over the leading of the Holy Spirit. No one has the right to tell a parent that what they feel the Holy Spirit is leading them to do is wrong—*unless* it is against a Biblical principle.

In several years of counseling, I have listened to countless parents tell how they subjected their parental power to the opinion of another human being.

John Evans told such a story. John was and is a deacon in a solid, Bible-believing church. Along with his wife, they have successfully served God in that church while raising a family of three boys and a girl. These are committed Christian people, the kind every pastor needs to do the work of the church.

John was the leader in the home. They did not have any major problems with their four children until he and his wife went to hear a well-known speaker on the Christian family in a nearby city.

They were told in that meeting that they were not strong enough in their discipline. Not personally, of course, but that was the message to the audience, and it seemed to make sense to them. After all, most Christian parents feel like they could do a better job with their family. John was not quick to spank his children, choosing instead to mix spanking with privilege removal, extra chores, and less television time for disobedience or carelessness.

But now he was told that spanking was the *only* way to

22

discipline children. John recognized that he could have been wrong in using other methods, and while his kids were pretty good, maybe they could be better.

So John toughened up.

More spankings, less of other methods of child discipline.

And now John Evans is in my office, explaining how he feels like he is being too hard on his kids, and wondering if he has done the right thing.

I asked John how he felt about children and discipline, and how he felt about himself as a parent.

He answered that he used to feel pretty good about being a father, but now he was having some doubts.

As we talked, it became clear that this father was uneasy because he was doing something he did not feel right about. I suggested that, unless that feeling contradicted a scriptural principle, it was coming from the Holy Spirit who was trying to lead him in the right direction with the kids. His responsibility as a Christian parent was to listen to the leading of the Holy Spirit in those areas of child-rearing not specifically addressed in the Bible. It is one of the reasons God provided the Holy Spirit at Pentecost.

What a look of relief came over his face.

"You mean I don't have to discipline my kids the way that speaker said?"

I suggested that the speaker has no responsibility for John's children. He should discipline his children and lead his Christian life as *he* felt the Lord would have him to do.

Being a godly parent means that we are sensitive to the still small voice of God as He speaks to us about our children. We have the unchanging Bible to search. Three times the book of Proverbs warns us that "in the multitude of counsellors there is safety" (11:14; 15:22; 24:6). But when specific answers are not given, we can turn confidently to the Holy Spirit for guidance.

Power in Christian parenting results from being the kind of parent God would have us be. Power in Christian parenting is *knowing* what is expected of us. Power in Christian parenting works!

2
PARENT POWER LOSS

Many of the parents I see in my office are having trouble controlling the behavior of their children. The inability to control is a basic and troubling burden for parents, and ultimately boils down to a fundamental question of power.

Parent power always begins firmly fixed in the hands of new parents. Think of the totally helpless infant. Dependent on mother and father for 100% of survival needs, he is absolutely, unquestionably submissive to the will and power of his parents. The toddler is one who lives in a land of giants. His eyes focus on kneecaps instead of other eyes, and he must look up to nearly everyone—often even the dog!

The elementary age child is only a little bigger, and still surrounded by the realization of his own lack of knowledge in school. She is beginning to try to earn the smiles and compliments of her parents and teachers. And even the teenager, almost full-grown, is still mortifyingly self-conscious and desperately in need of the family car and gas money for that date next weekend.

These kids need us! How in the world did we become dependent on them, and how did they get the idea they could disobey us?

As we try to answer these questions we need to remember that parents do not *lose* power. We give it away. We surrender to the demands of time and expediency; we capitulate to the strategy of whine and pester, pout and tantrum, because it is just easier. For now! But slowly our compromises, our surrender of authority for *our* convenience, gives our power away. We make the kind of statements that tell our kids, "Go ahead, take my authority, I'm not using it anyway."

For example:

"Don't bother me right now. I don't care what you watch on television."

—*Subtract two power units*—

"I don't have time to talk to you about your grades right now. Just try to do better."

—*Subtract three power units*—

"Well, if Susan's parents are letting her go, I guess its okay for you to go, too."

—*Subtract two power units*—

"Stop crying! I guess one cookie before dinner won't do any harm."

—*Subtract five power units*—

"Oh, let him stay up for awhile. Those tantrums are really getting me down."

—*Subtract four power units*—

"Ask your mother. If it's okay with her, it's okay with me."

—*Subtract two power units*—

"I suppose if all your friends are wearing purple and green hair, it's okay for you."

—*Subtract three power units*—

"Okay, okay. If you'll just stop crying while we're in the store, you can have the candy bar."

—*Subtract four power units*—

"If the school says that music is acceptable, I guess it's all right for you to listen to it."

—*Subtract five power units*—

"I'll check with the pastor and see what he thinks."

—*Subtract five power units*—

I don't suppose anyone knows how many power units we have when a child comes into a family, but if we do enough of this, they can't last very long. We relinquish our parent power to the school, the pastor, the other kids, other parents, the media, and mostly, to our own children. And getting power units back is like pulling teeth. Having power is fun, and almost everyone who has some wants to keep it. Parent power units, of course, is simply an attempt to convey the idea of a

25

quantity of power given to parents by the Lord. Parent power loss is an unnecessary draining away of godly influence on children.

A teenager is probably going to approach power units a little differently. Adolescents see power in terms of precedent. "If you gave me permission to go to a movie last week, it must be all right to go to one this week," they will tell parents. Once the gap between "no movies" and "some movies" is breached, it's breached for good. Beware of precedent setting!

But parent power is never truly lost because we always know where it is. It's just that it no longer resides with the parent. We scatter our power around to those who are usually very willing to take it from us and use it for us. A chart of one parent's power might look like this:

Location of Parent Power Units	
Location	Amount
teacher	8%
pastor	12%
child's friends	10%
friend's parents	3%
television	15%
child	20%
grandparents	10%
other relatives	7%
parents	15%

No wonder we can't get our kids to do what we want them to do! I couldn't even lift a bologna sandwich if all I had was 15% of my physical strength. Can we really be surprised when a child in this situation says "no" or goes out and does what he wants anyhow? Who would respect a policeman who was only 15% as tall or as strong as he should be? Who would hire a worker who could only work at 15% productivity? What a mess this power shortage can produce!

Power Outages

There are both voluntary and involuntary drains on parent power. We have just looked at some of the more-or-less voluntary ways of surrendering our power. I want to turn now to involuntary power loss. I've called these "power outages" because of their situational and usually involuntary natures. Perhaps we can visualize the process this way.

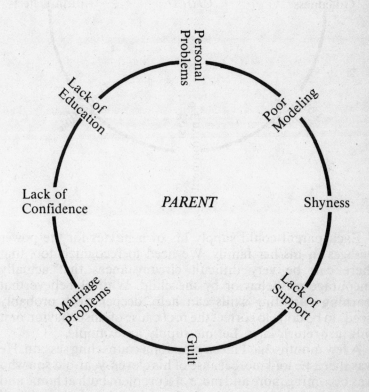

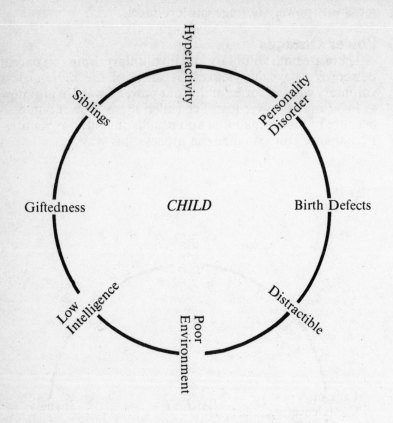

Each parent could supply his own names for the power outages in his/her family. We need to recognize, too, that there can be very difficult circumstances that actually encourage misbehavior by the child. While I believe that learning parenting skills can help, deeper work probably needs to be done to correct the root cause of misbehavior, or it will just return later. Let me supply an example.

A few months ago I met a man for a counseling session. He was there, he told me, because of his eleven-year-old son who was becoming more and more of a problem both at home and school. Ricky had acquired what his father called a "bad attitude." Ricky's teachers agreed. Ricky's parents had been divorced for about three years. The father was only sporadically employed, but for some reason had custody of Ricky, his brother (9), and his sister (8).

Money problems had forced Ricky and his family to move into a mobile home with Ricky's grandmother, a divorced lady herself with one teenager still at home. It turns out that Ricky, his dad, his brother, and his sister all had to sleep in one room and *in one bed!* There was no privacy in the trailer and only one bathroom. The terribly cramped living conditions created bickering and general unhappiness. Ricky started acting out at school following the move to the mobile home.

I explained to Ricky's dad that while I could offer some suggestions, any child living in those conditions would become angry and frustrated, inevitably showing it in some way. I felt that he was taking out his anger on his teachers and schoolmates. I told the father that unless the living arrangements changed, there was very little anyone could do over the long run.

In this case, Ricky's dad lost his parent power through circumstances largely beyond his control. In other situations, the cause might be illness, unemployment, marital difficulties, or any number of other reasons. They could all be parent power outages, and they may be uncorrectable. We have to recognize these circumstances for what they are. They are problems requiring a deeper level of help than just wanting to do better.

Finding the Power Outage

Working with the parents of misbehaving children has shown me the need for a way to identify the specific source of power loss. I am going to suggest a couple of methods that have worked reasonably well for me. The first is one I call the Aggravation Scale.

29

Aggravation Scale

Check the following behaviors that occur with your child. Then rank them from (1) most important to (15) least important. You do not have to check every choice.

_____ 1. Temper tantrum

_____ 2. Talking back

_____ 3. Whine

_____ 4. Direct disobedience (doing other than commanded)

_____ 5. Demanding parent's attention (interrupting other conversations, etc.)

_____ 6. Shouting

_____ 7. Aggressions (hitting, biting, etc.)

_____ 8. Humiliates (puts others down)

_____ 9. Destructive behavior (breaking toys)

_____10. Non-compliance (failure to do as commanded)

_____11. Cursing (vulgarities and profanity)

_____12. Teases and aggravates others

_____13. (Fill in your own)_____

The aggravation scale works best when dealing with younger children who are in and around home most of the time. This device allows parents to clarify their own thinking in terms of exactly what it is that aggravates them most. Work can then begin on the most serious perceived problem.

Another way to examine a particular misbehavior closely is with the A-B-C-D coding form. It might look like this for a seven-year-old boy.

A-B-C-D FORM

Antecedent Conditions	Behavior	Consequences	Discrimination/ Learning
Riding in family car on the way to church	Refused to sit still, cried, whined	Allowed to sit by window if quiet	Repeated behavior next day, got to sit by window again
In supermarket	Told "no candy," screamed and cried	Threatened, scolded, given candy when quiet	Repeated behavior at department store
In backyard with playmates	Used profanity	Spanked, warned	Did not repeat
Outside playing	Refused to come when called	Allowed to continue playing	Repeated refusals

Just a brief look will make clear that certain parent responses encourage bad behavior; other responses encourage good behavior. The utility of such a form is the easy clarification of cause-and-effect problem behavior and the realization that power for good or bad behavior rests in the hands of parents.

Another form (remember, these are just examples) that has helped some parents get a handle on misbehavior is called the Behavior-Misbehavior Record Sheet. The advantage I have found with this form is its applicability to children of any age.

Behavior - Misbehavior Record Sheet

DATE	TIME	COMMAND	RESPONSE (child)	RESPONSE (parent)	FOLLOW-UP
11/15	6 p.m.	Don't drop food on the floor	behavior continued	spanks (6 times)	cried, promised not to repeat, repeated next meal
11/15	9 p.m.	Go to bed	cried, begged to stay up	ignored crying, put in bed and firmly warned	has not repeated
11/16	7:30 p.m.	Brush your teeth	non-compliance	threatened, told to go to bed early that night	claimed nausea, stayed home from school, whined
11/19	5 p.m.	Pick up your toys	obeyed	hugged, told "good boy"	asked if Mom needed help in kitchen
11/26	9 a.m.	Get ready for church	said O.K. but did not	told "no dessert at dinner"	cried at dinner, whined, got dessert
12/1	8 p.m.	Take your bath	cried, said didn't feel good enough	warned would have to go to bed early	bath taken
12/3	1 p.m.	Stop shouting	complied	told "good boy," hugged and praised	did not repeat

We could look at additional examples, but the point to be made is simply that children and adolescents need to know that their parents are in charge. We give our power away to our children and others by the way we respond to their responses. We give a command and expect that it will be responded to positively. When the response is not what we want, we need to back up and take a look both at our response and the way we gave the command in the first place.

Effective and Ineffective Commands

Sometimes we get into difficulty with discipline because of careless phrasing of commands. The following examples represent some of the common errors in command-giving by parents. Every parent does these once in awhile. But serious problems can result when we use a particular, ineffective command on a regular basis.

Togetherness Commands

"Let's clean up our room now."
or
"Are we ready for our bath?"
or
"Let's give Aunt Harriet a big hug."

Not only do togetherness commands confuse children, but they sound silly to anyone listening. Any child will know that only he is expected to clean his room, take a bath, or give Aunt Harriet a hug. Keep commands simple!

Commands with Explanations

"Clean up your room. Company is coming."
or
"Sit down! It's dangerous to stand up in a moving car."
or
"Go to bed now. We are leaving early in the morning."

Commands with explanations tell a child to obey a parent based on the reason given. The logical offshoot will be a child learning to say "why" after every parental command or to feel that obedience is not required if the rationale doesn't make sense to him. It is entirely possible that there will be times

33

when a quick response is needed for the safety of the child. We cannot allow automatic hesitation or questioning.

Vague Commands

"Be good at school today."
or
"Don't make a mess in the den."
or
"Stay close to home."

Ambiguous commands such as these simply allow too much leeway for individual child judgment of how good is good, what constitutes a mess, whether close to home means in the backyard, within shouting distance, or on the same continent. Once again, keep commands simple and specific.

Choice Commands

"How would you like to have a babysitter tonight?"
or
"I'll bet you would enjoy spending the day with your cousin Norman."
or
"Would you like to take your bath now?"

Even a child knows that when someone asks if you would like to do something, they mean for you to choose. So when given a choice, as in these examples, the child will assume you meant what you said. So when he responds, "No thanks, I'd rather eat worms than visit weird cousin Norman," don't be surprised.

Sequence Commands

"Finish your lunch, wash up, and then you can go outside after you have picked up your toys."

What a mouthful! And what an earful for a child to take in and remember all at once. Think of how it is for you at work when your boss gives you more that one set of instructions at a time, or when the doctor gives you four things to do for your child before he can return to school. Give one command at a time; wait for its accomplishment; then move on to the next.

Effective Commands

Good, effective parental commands are specific, direct, and clear. This means that we are to say exactly what is meant without embellishment. We should make eye contact with the child and hold it until the command is understood. I've yet to see a more or less normal child or adolescent who wasn't strongly influenced by a parent or teacher unafraid to hold eye contact. Use a firm, "I really mean it," voice, and give commands one at a time. When the command is given, stand still, and wait for the child to obey. Don't walk around or get busy doing something else. Act like you expect compliance *now!*

"John, pick up your toys, now!"
or
"Susan, if you do not get off the phone within 30 seconds, you are grounded tomorrow. One, two, ..."
or
"Bill, be in the house by 11:30 tonight without fail. Is that clear?"

Clear, direct, unambigous commands followed by parent behavior that communicates the expectation of obedience gets results. Prior thought and preparation can avoid a lot of hassles with our children.

As you work your way through this book, we will look at more specific causes of parent power loss as well as some specific remedies. We have only scratched the surface in our examination of power in Christian parenting, and I expect that there are a multitude of unanswered questions remaining.

But questions are the foundation of good Christian parenting. Without questions we would all be lost in our smug assurance that as long as we obey the jot and tittle of the law, our kids will turn out great. God did not make us puppets, but rather, free-thinking people with a free will who can determine to walk with God or in another direction. Your questions about children and parenting caused you to

35

acquire this book. Your questions about children will make it likely that you will actually find answers to your family concerns. These questions and the answers you find will make it possible for you to help other parents who have not found the answers yet.

Ephesians 4:1-3; Isaiah 40:29; Psalm 25:9 tell us that God respects meekness. We are to be meek as we recognize that God is the source of the answers we find and that He is the Creator of the mind that recognized the questions in the first place. Meek but not weak—because God is the source of our strength (Isaiah 12:2; Psalm 27:1, 73:26).

How have you stewarded the 100% power supply God gave you when your child was born?

How much do you want to get your authority back?

Chapter three begins the process.

3
RECONNECTING PARENT POWER

Is it ever too late?

Kevin's parents thought so, and I wasn't too sure they were wrong.

Kevin was a thirteen-year-old who seemed to have no regard at all for what was expected of him. His teachers were convinced he was incorrigible; his friends didn't come around very much anymore, and his parents were at the end of their rope, slipping fast. Kevin was on a path toward serious trouble, and all attempts at redirecting him had failed.

As I became more deeply involved in the counseling relationship with Jim and Marie, Kevin's parents. I began to realize that this kid had reason to be upset. Three years earlier the parents had separated. Kevin was only ten when Dad left, but he remembered that event. He recalled it to me in such vivid and angry detail that it was clear he had not even come close to forgiving his father for leaving. He was determined to get even with any adult who happened to be around.

And Kevin's anger continued even after Jim and Marie reconciled and put the family back together. It had been only three years without Dad in the home, but the damage to Kevin had been done. It didn't matter to Kevin that Mom and Dad had experienced a spiritual as well as a marital healing. All he knew was that he had been deprived of a dad at a time when all his friends had theirs, and he was mad about it!

In talking with Jim and Marie, I tried to make clear what Kevin was communicating to me about his anger and his sense of being rejected by his father. Marie was having an especially hard time understanding why Kevin was so upset with *her* since it was clear that the break-up was his dad's doing. Both Jim and Marie were dedicated to correcting what had gone wrong, but they couldn't get Kevin to work with them.

Was it too late for Kevin?

No, of course not. But just as the children are usually not consulted when parents split up, Kevin was not consulted about his parent's reconciliation. Marie might have been ready to take Jim back, but Kevin wasn't. And he was determined to stay that way.

In his book, *Why Children Misbehave,* Dr. Bruce Narramore says, "As long as children are in our home, we maintain an influence. It is true that children are more pliable in the first few years of life, but there is plenty of room for change." I needed to convince Kevin's parents of the truth of Dr. Narramore's statement.

What Jim and Marie needed to understand was that they had created the angry mindset in their son, and only time and calm, consistent love was going to change the damage three years had done. We worked very slowly with Kevin and his parents to reconnect their power base with their son. A foundation had to be rebuilt with love and care. Gradually both parents, but especially Jim, were able to exercise more and more control over Kevin's behavior. Now we are *almost* back to where the family was before the break-up.

But reconnecting parent power and influence is never as efficient as keeping the power lines unbroken from the beginning, a fact Jim and Marie will realize as time passes and Kevin grows.

Derivative Authority

We have all heard the old Negro spiritual that says, "The knee bone connected to the ankle bone; the ankle bone connected to the foot bone."

Well, in something of the same sense, we can understand the development of parent power as passing from one generation to the next but ultimately coming from God. John Whitehead, the well-known constitutional attorney who has battled mightily for the rights of Christian schools, says, "Parenthood requires a responsibility to handle the gift of children properly. This means that parents must perform specific duties toward their children. These duties stem from their derivative authority—derivative of the Creator" *(Parent Rights,* Crossway Books, 1977).

What John Whitehead seems to be saying is that the responsibilities we accept as Christian parents stem directly from God as our Parent. As God exercises power and influence on us, so we as parents are to exercise Spirit-led power and influence with our children. To resist the application of power in the family is to be outside the will of God. These powers derive from God as surely as our power as American citizens derives from our Constitution. Godly power and influence are indispensable if a family is to honor God; they are every bit as indispensable as love. For love that doesn't care enough to protect and nurture cannot be true love.

Parent Guilt

A major reason Jim and Marie were powerless with their son Kevin was the guilt they felt for the temporary break-up of their marriage. Kevin sensed that guilt and sought to exploit it. To restore essential power to Kevin's parents meant that somehow we had to confront their guilt.

Dealing with guilt that is unjustified and without foundation is one thing, but trying to deal with guilt that is deserved is another story altogether. Even though Jim and Marie had confessed their sin to God and were sure they were forgiven, the fact that Kevin was unwilling to forgive them continued to present problems. I knew that until Kevin's parents could act on their forgiveness to Kevin, through their behavior, the battle would continue.

Experience shows that once parents stop accepting guilt for a real or imagined error, children eventually catch on and stop trying to exploit that guilt. But if parents are unwilling or unable to accept the forgiveness of God *and continue to act guilty,* the children will continue their attempts to control the family.

Parents in a guilt-produced predicament with their children need only confess their sin to God and ask His forgiveness. Once this is done, we are to believe what God has promised and stop acting like we are still unforgiven. If the children have been offended or injured, as in Kevin's case, parents should ask the forgiveness of the child or teenager. It is a humbling but essential part of the healing process.

But when it's over, it's over. Move on. Children and teenagers will often repeat their attempts at resurrecting the guilt in hopes of getting something they want, but consistent parental behavior will win out. Remember, behavior that is not reinforced always dies out eventually.

Parenting Style

Diana Baumrind, development expert and a well-known authority on parenting, suggests the existence of three distinct styles of parenting. Each of the three methods has ramifications for the use of power in families as well as impacting the ability to reconnect parent power once it is lost.

It is important to recognize that most children are parented by two parents, each from a different background and family, and each bringing to the marriage their own set of attitudes and beliefs about how to raise children. The point is that there are no pure types, no 100% anything in parenting. We are all combinations of what we have learned and experienced from life in general, and what we gained by being raised by the parents God gave us.

Having said all this, and in hope of reducing the temptation we all seem to have to put things into absolute categories, let's look at the three parenting styles Baumrind suggests.[1]

The Authoritarian Parent

Parents dominated by an authoritarian attitude about child–rearing attempt to shape, control, and evaluate the behavior and attitudes of their child. This conforms with a set standard of conduct, usually based on absolute and legalistic standards. Such parents usually value obedience for its own sake. When infractions and misbehavior occur, they tend to employ harsh, forceful, and punitive methods to curb self-will in the child.

Authoritarian parents emphasize the value of authority

and tradition in politics, religion, *and* child-rearing practices. There is very little conversation between parent and child or parent and teenager in authoritarian families because children and teenagers are seen as having very little of value to offer in an adult discussion.

Authoritarian families often come from a military background or a strict religious orientation. Authoritarian parents tend to produce very well behaved children and problem teenagers.

Power and influence in authoritarian families is based on rank, size, age, or some other quantifiable measure. When the children grow to such a size that intimidation is less and less effective with each passing year, the family structure crumbles. Everyone reading this book probably knows at least one family similar to what I've just described and whose children rose up in rebellion during adolescence and left the home, usually under negative circumstances.

Authoritarian families have a very strong power cord attached to each child, but the cord isn't very long. As the children grow, the cord is stretched and stretched until, when it breaks, it often breaks for good. Authoritarian families frequently have problems dealing with teenagers and young adults because the power they exercised on their children was not godly power.

People who grow up in authoritarian homes often feel protected and cared for but not loved. When God expresses His love to us, He is not coercive. We can accept His love or reject it. In authoritarian homes, the children have no choice. These children are forced to obey, forced to respect their parents and other adults, forced to submit their wills to that of their parents. Because the freedom to choose obedience is totally stifled in these families, when the youngsters grow to young adulthood and experience their first opportunity to choose for themselves, they tend to choose something other than what was forced on them all those years.

When power is disconnected in authoritarian families, the break is more permanent and more severe than in any other. It is a major undertaking to try and reconnect power in an authoritarian family.

The Permissive Parent

Permissive parents tend to see their role as that of leader rather than dictator, a consultant instead of an absolute authority. Permissive parents usually behave in a non-punitive, accepting, and affirmative manner toward their children. Children and teenagers are brought into family discussions about where to spend a vacation and whether the family rules need adjusting.

Rather than attempting to shape and control the children, as is the case in authoritarian families, permissive parents allow the children to regulate their own behavior as much as possible. Where the authoritarian parent might say, "Bed time is ten o'clock on school nights until the tenth grade," the permissive parent is likely to say, "Stay up as late as you like as long as you can get up in the morning and don't fall asleep in school."

When disciplinary matters come up, permissive parents are much more likely to use reason rather than threats or force to get compliance. These parents tend to make few demands on the kids for chores and other responsibilities, believing that motivation for a clean room or well-pressed clothes must come from within the child rather than the parent.

Permissive parents often have better control of their children and teenagers than the more coercive authoritarian parents, but power and influence are not as obvious. Whereas the power cord is strong but short in authoritarian families, in permissive families, it is much weaker but more flexible and capable of stretching great distances without breaking. Permissive parents have an easier time raising children, and research tends to support the notion that of the extremes of authoritarian and permissive, the latter produces better adult children.

The Authoritative Parent

Finally, we come to the model of parenting that most closely resembles that found in the Bible. We know that God neither bludgeons us into accepting His salvation nor is careless about its availability to us. In Him we see the authoritative parenting style in which one attempts to direct a child's behavior in a rational, sensible, issue-oriented manner that encourages verbal give-and-take on family matters.

In contrast to authori*tarian* parents, authori*tative* parents value expressions of independence, both in terms of autonomy and voluntary conformity and discipline. These parents will use reason *and* power to achieve objectives in the family. At points of divergence, parental authority prevails.

Where permissive parents might give too much leeway to the child or teenager, the authoritative parent recognizes that both parent and child have rights in the family. Authoritative parents seem to be the most adept at applying the principles contained in the verse, ". . . as for me and my house, we will serve the Lord" (Joshua 24:15).

Authoritative parents have a power source that connects directly to God. That power cord is linked to the children in such a way that it is not noticed very often, being soft and comfortable in the way it is attached to the child. It is strong enough to restrain the child when needed, but it is long and flexible enough to remain part of the person throughout life, although it is barely noticed.

Authoritative parents produce the best adult children, according to the experts. And most Bible authorities agree that this is the kind of parenting taught in Scriptures.

Your Style of Parenting

I heard someone say that if both parents always agree, one of them is unnecessary. If you have a spouse to share your parenting responsibilities, expect to disagree often about the children. But never argue or debate about the children in front of the children. It is absolutely essential that no matter what particular style of parenting is practiced in your family, the children must always see a united front from their parents.

Your style of parenting will be a combination of these we have discussed. Accept the challenge to "search the Scriptures

43

daily" to see how closely you obey what God instructs in His Word. And if your parenting is not very effective right now, remember that there is a model available to you, but you must become familiar with the Word to know that model. As a personal testimony, I can affirm the authoritative model as that which is closest to what is found in the Bible. Your type of parenting will follow you and your children all your lives. It must not be taken lightly or for granted.

Meeting Basic Needs in Children

Power loss bears negative and unwanted fruit. But for every parent action, there is a child *re*action. When parents lose or surrender their power and influence with their children, for whatever reasons, the children in the family are bound to react. Expressions of non-control *threaten* children, and they are certain to react to that threat. Weak or ineffective parents produce fear in children. The fear that is produced can result in any number of negative reactions and behaviors. Powerless parents threaten the very survival of their children—in the child's mind at least. Children deprived of their basic security needs either seek security elsewhere or create problems for their parents in the hope of regaining the control they need in order to feel safe again.

Bobby

Moving to Virginia from California could be considered traumatic, depending on what one thinks of California as a place to live. But for eleven-year-old Bobby Clark, it became deep-rooted trauma. He had not objected to the news of his dad's transfer to the east coast. Even though Bobby's family had lived in California since before Bobby could remember, it didn't seem like a bad idea at the time.

But something changed in Bobby's mind during the move. The whole family moved together, even the dog. They moved into a great house in a very nice neighborhood, but something was bothering Bobby. He began having trouble sleeping, even waking up his younger brother across the room with his dreams, moaning, and groaning. More and more often he

44

complained about minor things like stomachaches and other minor aches and pains.

Mr. and Mrs. Clark came to see me about Bobby. As we talked, it became clear that they believed something about the move to Virginia had caused their son to begin acting this way. We discussed how the news of the move had been broken to Bobby and his brother, what questions they asked, and whether they seemed concerned about moving out of the only family home they had ever known.

However, we couldn't pinpoint anything—not until I listened more carefully to Mr. Clark talking about his job. Bobby's dad had attempted to rationalize the need for this move by telling the kids that he had no choice. It was not really true, but it apparently sounded good at the time. Mr. Clark left the impression with Bobby that the family was at the mercy and whim of Mr. Clark's boss, a man Bobby had never met.

Suddenly, there it was!

The thought in Bobby's mind, that was rapidly becoming an obsession, was that the Clark family could be uprooted again if his dad's job demanded it. Mr. Clark had committed one of the cardinal sins of parenting. He had assumed that children automatically understand what adults are talking about. In allowing Bobby to get the impression that the Clark family were virtual slaves to his dad's employer, Mr. Clark was telling Bobby he was too weak and powerless to be the dad Bobby had always thought him to be.

Bobby's security and sense of belonging had been secretly threatened, not by the move itself, but by what the move represented. The fact that he believed his dad didn't have a choice about moving was terrifying to Bobby. The unspecific physical problems and sleep disturbances were a direct result of the loss of security Bobby felt when faced with the reality of a weak parent.

Counseling with Bobby confirmed the problem. Just a few family sessions were enough to reassure Bobby that his dad could quit or refuse to move if he wanted, and no one could force him to do anything he didn't want to do.

Mr. Clark had his parent power back; Bobby had his security restored, and all was right with the Clarks' world again.

The Need for Security

God ordained the family as the framework for raising children. The family unit of parents, children, and sometimes grandparents, too, is essential. Security is feeling safe and protected; it is knowing that Mom and Dad will be there when you wake up in the morning, and that someone will be there when you get home from school. Feeling secure is knowing that there is no monster too big for Mom and Dad to handle, no bully too big to be chased off, and no robber so sneaky as to be able to break into the house where *your* Mom and Dad live.

Feeling secure is great!

Security was and is God's plan for the family. But statistics tell us that as of 1990 almost 45% of all children will have spent at least part of their growing up years without a dad in the home. From Mother we get love and nurture, the sense of being special and cared for, but Dad makes us feel safe. When Dad leaves for any reason, security goes with him.

Feeling insecure is terrible!

And it is possible for a father to leave without leaving physically, at least in the child's mind. Dad can abandon the family by not caring about the family members, not spending time with the kids, and by not being strong.

A weak father threatens the security of his children. A weak father tells his children that they *do* have something to worry about, that there is, in fact, a threat to their safety and security, that there are monsters out there Dad can't fight off.

That's what Bobby Clark thought. He thought his dad was too weak to fight off his monster boss who was making the family move to Virginia against their will. Security is so basic that every Bobby Clark in the world would have the same reaction to the thought that his father was unable to protect him.

If you wish to reconnect your parent power, Dad *or* Mom,

you must convince your children that you care enough about them to fight off any "monster" that could come along—no matter what. To reconnect your power, you must let God lead you in making the right decisions about plugging in your power cord to your children's lives. Then once the decision is made, you should sit down with the children and tell them what you have done. Tell them that you have an absolute commitment to them, and you are not going to do anything that would harm them. Tell them that you are there to help them grow, and, *no matter what*, you will not change your mind. Tell your children, as Mr. Clark did, that by God's grace and in His power, their parents will be there to care for them as long as they need it.

Feeling secure is a tremendous emotion—for children *and* parents!

Angela

Freshman college students have a multitude of hurdles to clear in that first traumatic year away from home. Angela seemed to be adjusting better than most to the freshman experience. She was the only child of an upper middle class family from Ohio. Both parents were college educated and Angela's mom had worked outside the home since Angela was a small child. Angela wasn't sure why she was an only child, but she suspected it was a choice her mother and father had made rather than a medical problem of some kind.

Angela was very attractive, if a little thin, had straight A's in high school and seemed to be on the same path in her first-year classes at the Christian college. There were dates in abundance for her, but she limited them to weekends because of studying, a revolutionary idea for most freshmen. It seemed to be a totally rosy picture for Angela, at least in the beginning.

As her classes progressed and the papers, tests, and assignments became more frequent, Angela began to change in subtle ways. Her roommates noticed that she was not eating regular meals, was refusing snacks completely, and even seemed to be throwing up without being sick. Her weight, which had always been on the low side, was dropping rapidly.

Angela was encouraged to visit the campus counseling center for an evaluation. She was also required to go in for a physical prior to her appointment.

You've probably guessed by now that Angela was becoming anorexic, another adolescent victim of self-starvation and the perfection syndrome.

As Angela progressed in counseling with one of the female counselors on staff, she began to understand about her extreme dieting and her compulsive need to be perfect in every way, including being "perfectly" thin. It seems that Angela's mom had always stressed that girls are smarter than boys, cleaner than boys, and more moral than boys. Angela learned at a very early age that if she was to keep her mother's love, she had to be perfect.

In childhood, perfection was all A's and never getting dirty. In adolescence, it was all A's and never getting into trouble. Now in college it was all A's and never causing problems for the parents who were paying for her education.

But when her all A's started to include an occasional B, Angela felt like a failure. Her attempts at perfection had met a roadblock called Biology 101 and her weight loss, her anorexia, was to make up for the B in biology.

Angela felt she needed to earn love from her parents, and if she couldn't get straight A's, she had to find something else to do. Weight loss was her way of earning love. Her mother had always despised overweight people, calling them undisciplined and lazy.

Angela had mis-learned the meaning of love and how it is acquired, only counseling could change her misconception. Fortunately, counseling did help Angela deal with her feelings in a more constructive way. She will always be thin and perfectionistic probably , but we don't expect her to get sick again.

Angela thought that her mother's love for her was a *conditional* love, a love based on performance rather than personhood. Angela struggled with perceived failure because

48

getting B's meant that her mother would not love her *unless* she made up for the B in some other way. Lower grades meant lower value to her parents, at least in Angela's mind. This was so scary to her that she *had* to find some other way to earn the love she needed.

Unconditional Love

The kind of love Angela experienced was conditional love–miscommunicated by her parents. In this case, their parent power was lost through communicating, however unconsciously, that their love was performance based and could be taken away if she behaved badly enough. It makes little difference if that was the message that was intended. Most parents do not seem to realize the content of these messages at the time they are sent. But if you have received comments from your children or teenagers indicating to you that *they may* feel this way, something must be done to correct that wrong impression. Extra measures of affirmation, encouragement, hugs, non-judgmental acceptance are places to begin.

We know that God loves us unconditionally. He hates sin but loves sinners. Unfortunately, it is a truth that is very hard to accept by someone seeking God's forgiveness.

Your child is not likely to be "deep" in sin, but an over-strict or legalistic environment can make kids feel like they are much worse than they are. Conservative Christians, especially, have a tendency to over-control and are prone to becoming legalists when the kids become teenagers. We do this because we love them, but the message they receive is that they must *earn* our continued love. Sometimes parents even say, "If you really loved me, you wouldn't get in trouble at school. Don't you know how embarrassing it is for us to have to go to the principal's office and bail you out?"

Messages like this tell the kids that we love them, otherwise we wouldn't bail them out of trouble, *but* that the love is conditional in the sense that we love them *more* when they are good. God does not love us more when we are good. We love *Him* more when we are good. Children, including teenagers, who believe they are loved by parents conditionally tend to become frightened over the possibility of losing the love they need so much. This fear can have disastrous results.

Youngsters who experience conditional love tend to show one of two extremes of behavior. One: they become lap-dogs, doing almost anything to please their parents in deadly fear of doing something wrong that will confirm their greatest fear, losing a parent's love. Or, two, they become rebellious, conscious of their inability to be as good as they think they need to be, and unable to handle the fear. So they rebel, run away, fight back, and confirm what they believe to be their parents' negative expectations of them.

We lose parent power with our children if we offer them only conditional love. To correct problems and prevent further damage, sit down with your children one at a time, and tell each how you, as a parent, feel about him/her! It can be truly amazing how quickly some problems vanish just because a child comes to believe he or she is now loved *unconditionally.* Teenagers especially need this. They may not respond immediately or visibly, boys have special difficulties expressing their feelings, but it will show up in their behavior.

Unconditional love models the love God has for *all* people, not just the good ones. After all, Christ died for His enemies (Romans 5:8). Even so, we can express unconditional love to our children without compromising our beliefs or our testimony to others. While there may be a few children who would exploit this kind of a change in parents, eventually the need to prove the parent's seriousness will wear off. The child will settle down and relax, confident that he is loved and no longer needs to challenge parents to see if it is true.

Douglas

There is a saying to the effect that, "Parents are people too!" Well, children are people, too, with many of the same needs as adults—including the need for power. Douglas, an eighteen-year-old first-year student at a small Christian college, was really struggling with the issue of power.

Douglas was away from home for the first time and was finding his new independence a little difficult to handle. I came into contact with him after some minor scrapes with the school rules, and after receiving a letter from his parents. They asked me to see if I could help him make the adjustment to college a little more smoothly than he had done so far.

This young man was from what seemed to be an outstanding Christian family. Both parents were college graduates and very successful in different professions. Douglas and his fifteen-year-old brother were good athletes and at the top of their classes academically. Doug's testimony in his home church was impeccable, and he seemed to be above the level of most other freshmen spiritually.

So why was he having trouble living within the rules at school, rules that were more lenient than those he had grown up with? It didn't make sense to his parents, and even Douglas didn't seem to have a clue as to why he was misbehaving.

As we talked at the request of his parents, it became clear that he was happy with his parents; he respected and loved them; he appreciated their sacrifice in putting him through college, and that his spiritual life was genuine.

What was missing?

After much discussion over many days, I began to realize that the missing component in Doug's life was power. Not the overt kind of power that comes with being rich and able to do as one pleases, but the power to have a say in what becomes of one's life.

Douglas was raised in a good home with good parents who loved him very much. In fact, they loved him so much that they were afraid he would make a mistake if they left him alone to make his own decisions. So they made his decisions for him, right up until the time he went away to school. The absence of power in this young man's life was only now beginning to show up in his mild misbehavior. My job in counseling became that of exploring with Douglas the reasons for his parents' attitudes and how their behavior was still controlling him even though he no longer lived at home.

Power

Every human being needs to feel powerful! Every human being needs to have a sense of influence on others and on self. People need the Lord, a popular song says, but people also need to feel free to *choose* the Lord. We are not puppets nor robots.

Douglas's parents chose to keep power from their son in hopes of protecting him from the very real dangers of the world. Their motivations were the best; their methods were not so great. What Doug's parents forgot was that God built into each of us the basic needs that will draw us to Him eventually. These needs are often diverted by the pull of the world and its influence, but the needs are foundational and God-given.

When we deal with children, especially teenagers, we must meet their needs for power just as we meet their needs for unconditional love and acceptance in the family. Power is no less an important need than the others mentioned; it just frightens parents more.

Parents meet their children's needs for power by listening to them when they offer opinions, by considering their wishes when making family choices (e.g. vacation destinations), by letting them help in selecting their clothing and hair style, and by giving them small, but increasingly important personal decisions to make.

Power is the freedom to make decisions, but we sometimes forget that decision-making is an acquired skill, not an inborn ability. Young children and teenagers can be given power in totally harmless ways, but the feeling of having some influence in the family is very important. I have yet to work with a seriously disobedient or rebellious child from a Christian family who was able to exercise some control over his own life. In fact, the opposite is always true. Show me a seriously misbehaving youngster, and I'll show you a kid who feels powerless!

If this description sounds a little like your family, it is easily corrected. Talk things over with *all* the kids. Tell them what you are thinking, that maybe you have gone overboard in trying to protect them, and you want to start showing the confidence you have had in them all along. Start with small decisions and be prepared for some mistakes and some setbacks.

Douglas improved once he came to understand his reasons for having trouble with the rules. It took several letters and many phone calls to convince his parents to begin letting go, but gradually they did. Douglas knows that his younger brother will have less trouble than he did because his parents are starting earlier with him.

Kevin, Angela, and Douglas each had parents who loved them but had lost their power to influence their lives. Reconnecting parent power is never easy, but the same love that pulled the power plug is capable of making the connection again.

Is it ever too late to reconnect parent power? No, I don't think so. It may be too late to correct some mistakes that were made, but it cannot be too late to prevent whatever future damage might occur. Love is able. Love is power-full.

FOOTNOTES:

[1] Baumrind, Diana. "Parental Disciplinary Patterns and Social Competence in Children," *Youth and Society,* 1978, Vol. 9, pp. 239-276.

4
POWER-PARENTING YOUNG CHILDREN

First gods

Parents are the first gods anyone ever knows. The experiences we have as young children with these all-knowing, all-seeing, and ever–present people called parents builds our future attitudes and relationships with the true God. Children raised by warm and loving parents grow to see God as a God of love. Children raised by harsh, punitive, and legalistic parents develop a mindset that defines God as harsh, punitive, and legalistic—a God to be feared more than loved. Children raised by parents who are in control of the family, in love with their children, not afraid to express it, and willing to show their competence through careful use of their parental power and influence develop children who learn to trust God for their daily needs.

But what of children raised by power-less parents? If we learn about God from our parents, what kind of God exists for the children of parents who are unwilling or unable to discipline and direct their children?

Weakness produces fear in young children. One of the most basic needs in children of all ages, but especially in young children, is the need to feel safe and secure. Parents who allow themselves to become incompetent in controlling the behavior of their children communicate to their children that they do not love them enough to work at helping them grow. Parents tell themselves that they do not know what to do, but, in reality, they are usually unwilling to learn what to do with children. Parents are all created equally ignorant about child-rearing. There is nothing in the biology of producing a child that carries with it the necessary knowledge for raising that child. All of us have to learn. The question that needs an answer is: Where does the knowledge come from?

Parenting knowledge comes from the education we are given, the experiences we share with others who have become parents ahead of us. Most importantly, though, we learn to be parents by being raised by parents. We learn to parent by being children.

While there is no surprise in this, I want to emphasize that what is learned can be unlearned. Both weakness and power are learned parent attributes. As we teach our children about God through the image of Him that we represent, our children come to believe God is weak or powerful depending on what *we* are like. But whereas God does not change, we often do—and often we *need* to change. Weak parents *can* learn to be powerful and influential with their children, but the re-learning must begin when the children are very small or as yet unborn.

Sam

The average, good-sized church normally has a few reasonably wealthy families among its membership. The Tillotsons were such a family. Sam was their only child, born to Joyce and Larry after many years of prayer and waiting on God.

The Tillotsons were good people. Faithful Christians who attended every service and supported the ministry with their finances as well as their time. Sam, who was fifteen when I met with him the first time for counseling, was an above average student and well liked by the other kids. This was a family that seemed to be moving through the Christian life with very few bumps along the way.

But Sam was troubled about something. He didn't show much about his concerns to others, and it took some time for me to get a handle on what was on his mind. But when I did, what came out surprised me.

Sam was scared. Frightened. No, he couldn't say what he was afraid of, but he knew the fear had become stronger over the last few years. Sam told me that he had felt a little afraid as far back as he could remember.

Here was a teenager who had everything going for him.

Some who knew the family thought he had *too much* going for him. Yet he was afraid and unhappy and growing more so every day.

What could Sam be afraid of?

After several weeks of counseling with Sam, it dawned on both of us that he was afraid of his parents, and most afraid of his father. Sam seemed as confused as I about why he was afraid, but there it was.

As we dug deeper, it began to make more sense. Sam had always been spoiled, over-indulged by otherwise good parents who showed their love for him in ways that seemed appropriate to them. The problems stemmed from the different perception Sam had of the reasons for being given virtually everything he wanted.

To this Christian young man, being spoiled meant that his parents felt that they had to *buy* his love, respect, and obedience. Sam believed that they loved him, but he couldn't understand why they felt such a need to, as he put it, "buy him off."

As it turned out, Sam was right. With his permission, I talked with his parents and gradually discovered that both of them, but especially Larry, were so afraid of alienating their son, of chasing him away somehow or of losing him to drugs or alcohol, that they tried to anticipate his every wish in hopes of heading off any serious problems. Larry had lost his fatherly power because of his fear of losing him. Sam sensed that lost power and interpreted it as meaning that he was not really loved.

After a few counseling sessions with all three members of the family, the issue was resolved, and Sam learned the reasons for his parents behavior. Each member of the Tillotson family achieved a new awareness of a godly use of power, and, while Sam was not necessarily thrilled by the new rules at home, he *did* feel more secure and protected knowing Mom and Dad loved him enough to tell him "no" at times.

Competence is Communicated
Even infants and young children are able to sense

emotional changes in the family before they are old enough to actually think about what is happening. We know that nursing mothers who are under a strain or experiencing some kind of anxiety have babies who are prone to be fussy and cranky. Experts tell us this is due to the baby feeling the tenseness in the mother's body while it is being fed.

Failure to Thrive Syndrome (FTTS) is an affliction of babies who are well-cared for physically but fail to grow properly. Often their mothers are young and unmarried. Failure to thrive babies are usually found in low income families with a relatively uneducated mother who is either afraid of hurting the baby or simply feels incompetent to care for it. The baby senses this feeling of anxiety in the mother and stops eating. These babies appear malnourished and wasted in spite of the fact that they are otherwise healthy.

Treatment for FTTS generally involves putting the baby in the hospital to regain its physical health while the mother attends group counseling sessions for new parents and takes some courses on parenting. Once she has learned enough to feel competent to care for her baby, and assuming the baby has regained its health and started to grow again, they return home and usually face no more problems in this area.

Competency is communicated, even to very young children and babies. What a young woman is given through the methods I just outlined is a sense of *power,* a feeling that she is strong enough and knowledgeable enough to raise her child properly. Power takes many forms, but it absolutely must be present in a family. When the absence of power is sensed, it seems to generate a sense of hopelessness and despair that, left uncorrected, often results in the death of a FTTS baby.

Building Our Power Base

Since even very young children and babies sense power and competence in their parents, let's look at parental behaviors that communicate the good feeling of being loved to a child.

Beginning at the beginning, babies under three-months-old need to experience the security of parents who provide smooth routines for them. Predictability is the key here. Having a mom and dad who respond and interact with the new baby gradually establishes the first level or parent power he feels.

From three months to about six months, the issue becomes how the baby deals with tension. It is during these months that the baby experiences his or her first frustrations. *The rattle has fallen out of the crib; Mom isn't coming when I cry, and nobody seems to know I'm a prisoner in this room.* But when Mom does come and talks to the baby, changes the eternal diaper, and produces food, the tension goes away. Babies at this age sleep about sixteen hours a day, so the tension can't be too overwhelming. What the baby needs from the caregiver at this time is simply sensitive, cooperative interaction when requested.

Between six months and a year, babies are well into making a firm emotional attachment to Mom. Dad comes later. This attachment is called bonding and is made possible through responsive availability. Experts tells us that it is virtually impossible to spoil babies younger than seven months, and we have learned that babies who are responded to more quickly, cry less often. It seems that there is some psychological testing going on in which the baby cries to see if Mom (or anyone) will respond. When the baby learns that they will be responded to, they ease up on the demands. Babies who are not responded to keep trying—and crying.

Beginning at 12 months we realize we have created a toddler, a small person capable of opening doors but incapable of closing a mouth. It is during the time between one year and 18 months that the toddler begins to explore seriously. Mom and Dad need to provide a secure base from which their toddler can experience the world . Parents must be careful to resist the temptation to over-control because too much control can frighten the toddler away from trying new things, an ability that is very important to the child's mental development.

Just a word on discipline. It is usually during this time that we first confront the need to discipline. Keep in mind, as you prepare yourself for this, that you are dealing with a *very* immature brain at this point, one incapable of understanding many things older children grasp easily. If you are satisfied that the child is willfully disobeying you, go ahead and discipline. *But,* be very careful to be gentle and considerate of the small size and small understanding of the toddler. Just a little slap or a loud word will be enough usually to discourage children of this age from continuing their experiment with disobedience. More on this later.

From 18 months to about 30 months, the child experiences the "terrible twos and threes." The reason these months seem terrible is that a normal child is attempting to establish a sense of individuality. Parents can recognize these times for what they are and *not* overreact with punishment. This child is exploring limits and will need to have some boundaries defined. We need to see his "No's" as normal attempts to discover the boundaries for himself. Parents can provide firm support and discipline without smothering normal curiosity and the need for independence. Firm support with much understanding is the key to surviving the terrible twos and threes.

And, then, during the preschool years, parents recognize that the child's understanding has dramatically increased and with it has come the need to make sexual identification and to establish relationships with age-mates. Parents now show their power and influence with the child by establishment of values and role expectations that the child is expected to accept and internalize. Parents demonstrate benevolent power to the child through their love, concern, and control and can fully expect that the child will transfer these behaviors to teachers and friends.

In each stage, parents are in charge. In each stage of preschool development, parents are free to exercise their power and influence with the child, knowing that this will eventually become a major part of the child's value system. The child thinks, "My parents love me enough to tell me "no" sometimes. I guess God cares for me at least as much as my parents, and so I know I can trust Him to care for me." Power, earthly and heavenly, is communicated.

Personality and Temperament

There are many common misconceptions about parenting. One of the more common is that all babies are alike. Well, not *really* alike, but not very different in any important way. The differences only start to show up as they get older.

But scientific research has shown that babies are *very* different, even at only a few days old. We have been able to identify three broad areas of difference in very young infants. These are termed difficult, slow-to-warm-up, and easy babies. From just a few days or weeks, nursery workers in hospitals have been able to predict what the newborns would be like as children, and they have been correct to a surprising degree.

Another study was done to see if more specific areas of difference could be found. After much careful research, it was shown that there are actually nine different areas that can be identified. By the age of two months, infants can be classified accurately as high, medium, or low on these behaviors: (1) Level and extent of physical activity. (2) Eating, sleeping, and toileting rythyms. (3) Withdrawal or approach in new situations. (4) Adaptability to change. (5) Sensitivity to stimuli. (6) Intensity of response. (7) General mood or disposition. (8) Distractibility. (9) Attention span.

Do temperament and personality exist in babies?

Absolutely!

Remembering that knowledge is power, parents who can recognize and deal with these differences in each child as they grow up are going to feel more competent and act more competently in raising that child. These differences illustrate why it is so important to have flexible rules and limitations that can be adjusted to meet the differing needs of our children.

Socialization in Early Childhood

Power in Christian parenting is expressed in many ways, but one primary expression of our parental influence with our children is how we civilize them. Psychologists would rather use the world "socialize," but because Christians value moral behavior very highly, "civilize" seems to fit.

We civilize our children primarily by how we raise them and what kind of examples we are to them. One of the major theorists and researchers in this area is Erik Erikson.[1] He was a student of Sigmund Freud who separated from his teacher over the importance of sexuality.

Erikson suggests that there are about ten goals to seek for our children. If these goals are reached, good personality development is assured. If not, problems will follow. Remember that this is one man's theory. We should not take it as absolute truth, but perhaps we can learn something about power-full parenting from it.

Children must develop an appropriate dependence-independence pattern of relationships. This means parents should help a young child become less driven by the need to be the center of attention by developing a sharing attitude. At the same time, it is important to encourage physical independence without losing emotional dependence in young children.

Second, socializing children means that we help them learn how to both give and take appropriate expressions of emotion. Clearly, most children learn this simply by observing their parents. But if a child leans toward one extreme or another, we are not just to leave the child alone to suffer the consequences. At the same time we are working on emotional expressions, the child must learn to deal with different social groups than he has known before. This becomes a dominant concern when the child starts school, but working on this ahead of time can be of extreme benefit to the young child.

Another very important aspect of becoming civilized has to do with authority. Every child has to deal with authority figures eventually, even if the parents are permissive in their methods. Children need to be able to take direction without resentment or disobedience. Along with this ability, the young child must learn both physical and emotional self-control. Children lacking in this kind of control are headed for a life of misery and rejection unless someone else steps in to help.

We will say more about sex-role later, but Erikson includes this as a major goal and an important aspect of becoming civilized as well. Part of sex-role is adjusting to one's changing and growing body, and Erikson even mentions the importance of learning modesty at an early age. I think most will agree that sexual modesty is an important part of being civilized, but isn't it strange how many adults have forgotten the modesty they learned in childhood?

We also expect the child to become less egocentric and learn to see self as one part of God's world and universe, but not the only part, as very young children tend to believe. The physical environment needs adjusting to as well as the world of language and thought.

Erikson supplied us with a long list, but it is easy to see the importance of the parent's role in the process of civilizing young children. I hope you see how important *you* are to your young child in these areas. Unfortunately, many parents have bought the idea that children are better off if left to themselves. This is a tragic error for any parent to make, but especially so for Christian parents.

How Young Children Think

We really have very little idea about the subject matter of the thoughts of babies. We know they think because of how they react to us. But beyond that, we are pretty much in the dark.

Preschoolers, however, are not so mysterious. We know that young children have significant ability to think, but we also know there are limitations on the thought capabilities of young children. It is here we will begin.

Young children are blessed with language and memory and other less distinctive abilities. But a part of using these abilities includes dealing with some limitations. These limitations include *animism,* the notion that all things are alive and have intentions and feelings. A small child might wonder if the car that has just been in an accident feels bad. *Finalism* is the belief that everything is intentional, meant to accomplish some goal or objective. This is seen in the tendency of young children to be fatalistic in assuming that certain things were just "meant" to happen.

Artificialism is assuming that human beings made everything, a particular problem for Sunday School teachers charged with the task of teaching the creation story to preschoolers. Young children are also *egocentric,* assuming that Mommy knows the secret not yet told to them, and restricted by *centration,* the inability to consider more than one dimension of a thing at a time.

There are other limitations of less significance, but the point that needs to be made is that Christian parents, who would be as powerful and influential with their children as possible, must take into account the different levels of understanding available to children of different ages. Once again, knowledge is power and obviously good for the child.

Language

There are several theories of language development. Of course, most experts agree that language development begins in very early childhood, possibly even in infancy. The major theories agree as well on the very great importance given to modeling in learning language. It is on this point I want to dwell for a moment.

The ability to use language begins with reception. Children begin to speak because they have the ability to hear. Without hearing, a child receives no feedback from their early attempts at communication. Deaf children babble and coo like all babies, but at some point around three or four months, the babbling and cooing cease. A basic principle of learning is without reinforcement, so behavior stops. No payoffs, no performance.

Children with normal hearing speak as they are spoken to. Immature in the beginning, of course, but in only a few years a child can keep up with an adult conversation, hesitating only to ask the meanings for unknown words. Children with normal hearing learn to speak by listening to their parents. They use the words and phrases we use because that's all they have. To be sure, they will pick up a few words from the other kids in the neighborhood, but the basic word use, accents, unusual phrases, and terminology all come primarily from parents.

Christian parents have a special responsibility to watch their language in front of their kids. Of course we should watch our language anyhow, but the importance of being careful is magnified with kids around. I was reminded of this one Sunday driving home from the morning church service which, that particular day, had included everything but a wedding and a funeral. So I did a complaining act, grouching over how inconsiderate the pastor was for keeping us late and how easy it would be to keep the service to a reasonable length. (There was a Detroit Lions-Green Bay Packers game on.)

Once at home, my wife graciously suggested that I consider what my complaining sounded like to the kids. Here I was, always reminding them to be respectful in church, but complaining about the inconsiderate pastor.

She was right of, course, and I do *not* complain in front of the children anymore. But what a lesson that was for me! We had small children then, and if I had continued modeling that type of attitude, I could have really corrupted their attitudes about respect for God's house and the pastor.

Do you make negative comments about racial, ethnic, or religious groups? Is it possible to tell Catholic or Jewish jokes, and then expect our children to be able to witness to these folks about who Jesus is? How about Polish jokes or any of the multitude of other ethnic groups we often make the subject of a joke? We easily forget that our children are listening with immature ears and minds. We know we don't *really* mean all those things, but do they know that?

We don't need to know all the fine details of exactly how children learn to use language to recognize our responsibility to be careful of what we say within their hearing. The words we use around them become the substance of their thoughts. People think in words, and words can become self-destructive if we are not careful. Parent power is never used better than to control the language our children learn to use.

Independence Begins at Home

Do you think most Christian parents want their children to grow up to be independent? Sometimes I wonder if we really do.

I know we talk like we value independence in our children, but somehow independence always seems to become labelled as rebellion. As I counsel with parents of teenagers, I am impressed with the confusion about independence versus rebellion, and how often that confusion leads to real problems in some Christian families.

We'll look at adolescent independence and rebellion later, but, for now, I want to examine the earliest beginnings of independence. This is important for us because the pattern of independence is set very early, and it is *very* difficult to change later.

Several developmental experts have studied the origins of independence in children and have come up with some interesting findings. A number of these relate directly to the way many Christian families are living.

To begin, we know now that environmental stimulation in early childhood leads to greater independence as the children grow. Things we often take for granted have been shown to be important: Taking kids along when we go to the hardware store or the supermarket. Letting the little kids help some with yard or house work. Talking to the kids. All of these common, everyday happenings encourage the development of independence and their absence *discourages* the development of that same independence.

We also know that overprotection, sometimes called "smother love," stifles independence as much as rigid and inflexible rules and discipline do. On the other hand, proper discipline that is reasonable, firm, and consistent has proven to encourage independence in young children.

The researchers also found that self-confidence and self-assertiveness in parents is picked up by children and reveals itself in independence eventually. It is interesting to note that when self-confidence is lacking in parents, and becomes replaced with bribery for good behavior, children become *dependent* rather than independent.

Finally, it was discovered that when parents have values stressing individuality, self-expression, initiative, and independent thinking, the children respond by growing up with a greater degree of independence *if* the parents practice discipline as noted above.

I would challenge you to think through your attitudes about independence. Consider that for a person to live a truly Christian life, he or she must constantly rebel against the pulls and tugs of the world. Becoming a Christian is the most independent thing a person can do because it means turning one's back on the world and swimming against the tide. Conformists make very poor Christians generally. All of the great Christian leaders from the apostles to Moody and Spurgeon were men who had the strength to be independent from the world and choose the non-conformist path of following Jesus.

Do we want out children to be independent?

You bet we do!

Early Sex-Role Development

God intended children to have two parents, one of each sex. A fairly simple plan it would seem, but one that is becoming increasingly unusual as our world continues to degenerate.

The value of having a mother and a father extends far beyond just sexual development, and we will not attempt to touch all those areas in this chapter. I do want to emphasize the importance, the *factual* importance, of both parents being present in the years before the child starts school.

I have listened to fathers explain their reasons for taking a job that required them to be away from home during the week. These reasons have much variety in them, but a common theme seems to emerge when talking about young children. Dads often say, "Well, I don't want to be gone at all, but I would rather be gone when the children are little than when they are older. After all, everyone knows they need their mom the most when they are very young."

No questions about needing Mom, but Dad is needed, too,

and not just to fix the washing machine. Sexual identity is established during the years *prior* to the child starting school. This identity is not finished in these early years, but the foundation is laid. Let me suggest that the *worst* time for a father to be gone from the home is when the children, especially boys, are in the pre-school years. Dad may think that he will change his job and be at home more when the boys get into junior high and start playing football or other sports. The problem is, if Dad has been absent from the lives of his sons for most of their developmental years, many of these boys will not want to play football. If dad was not around much when his son was learning what it is to be male, the boy might rather learn to knit than to play ball! There is a strong correlation between the increase in the divorce rate in this country, the removal of the father in most cases from the home, and the increase in male homosexuality.

While the presence of a father is not as important to daughters as sons, research shows that girls deprived of a father often marry too young and are much more likely to have marital problems. There is a strong correlation between marital satisfaction and success for girls and the active presence of a father in their lives.

We will look at more specific areas of sexual development later. But for now, we need to emphasize the importance of the two parent family. If God allows circumstances where both parents are not available, such things as death or military service, then we can trust God to make up for what is missing. We need to make sure it isn't our choice to raise children without a dad, though.

Toilet Training

As we look at toilet training, we need to remember the principle of learning discussed earlier. Behavior that is rewarded will repeat; behavior that is punished or ignored will diminish.

With that in mind, we can take note of the fact that bowel and bladder control is one of the few things the child of two or three has absolute control over. We can force on them all manner of strange foods and activities, and they really have no choice but to comply. They must go where we take them and stay where we leave them. We dress them to please us, give them baths as often as we think necessary, and generally make all the decisions for them.

But consider the power of the potty chair. At some point, usually around two, children begin to realize that if they don't want to "go," *nobody* can make them. NOBODY! Think of this as the first real sense of power in a human's life.

So when toilet training a child, make it a pleasant experience, with lots of rewards and no punishments. You don't want your child to get the notion that he or she has a *weapon* that does not shoot blanks and cannot be controlled by parents. I have worked with families where this kind of a problem was created because of overly harsh toilet training, and you don't want that kind of trouble in your family.

So after saying all this, here are some hints to make toilet training easier and prevent parent power loss even in the earliest, simpler stages.

Make sure the child has a word to describe their need to eliminate. "Go potty" is usually sufficient. The potty chair should be pleasant, colorful, and comfortable. Motivation can be increased with immediate rewards of favorite books to help pass the time, praise, or food following successful attempts. Recognize, though, that toilet training should only be started when the child is eager and willing to "be more grown up."

Anticipate this need by listening and watching for signals (squirming, grunting). Gently ask the child at appropriate intervals if he has to use the potty. Make sure the child is ready for this kind of self-control. We know that children experience different rates of maturation, and there is *no* set rule for when to begin.

Allow the child to see same sex members of the family using the toilet. It is amazing how efficient this method is for those adults who can overcome their embarrassment.

At last, avoid negatives. Resist the temptation to be harsh or punitive when "accidents" occur, and do not threaten or moralize about the reasons for the accident. Be aware that bed-wetting is common and often occurs, especially for boys, until the fifth year. Try to keep in mind that toilet training is a phenomenon peculiar to westernized cultures like ours. There are people around the world who never know what toilet training is, yet somehow learn to control this part of their physical life.

Finally, when in doubt about what to do, ease off!

Day Care

Is it possible to maintain parent power when enrolling young children in day care?

This is an especially important question given the realities of our modern economy and the need to have both parents working. Perhaps you have noticed that fewer and fewer pastors are preaching against the evils of Mom working outside the home. The fact is that most mothers *will* work outside the home, and most will do so for the majority of their child-rearing years.

Whether or not this should be, day care is a fact of modern life, and we must find a way to deal with it. Providing a rationale for day care does not imply an endorsement of our present situation, but the reality must be faced.

Research shows that a carefully chosen and well run day care center can be an advantage to young children. We have found that in many families where mother stays at home, very little time is actually spent *with* the children in playing games, reading stories, and learning new things. Mom is usually very busy, and with just one or two small children, it is a full time job managing the home. Many mothers do an excellent job of setting aside a special time each day to play and work with the children, but the percentage is not great.

We know that children placed in a *good* day care, one that is well staffed and efficiently operated, tend to be more mature when entering kindergarten and are advanced in social *and* intellectual skills. We voluntarily placed our youngest child in a day care center three afternoons a week in order to get her ready for the transition to kindergarten. Many churches with

Christian day schools operate a four-year-old kindergarten, which is usually just a day care with an educational name.

Day care can be a good experience for children and need not produce guilt in parents who *must* work. Parents considering enrolling a child in day care need to check the following things to see if the center is suitable.

A trained and certified teacher in charge of the program is becoming more and more characteristic of good day care programs. The ideal ratio of adult worker to child (depending on the age of the children) is about seven or eight to one. Hygiene and sanitary facilities need to be checked, and separate bathrooms for boys and girls are a necessity. The director of the day care should be able to supply a parent with a lesson plan for the week's activities, and these activities should be structured around learning, not babysitting. Both inside and outside play facilities must be safe and well maintained with adequate supervision. Menus can be checked for nutritional value.

The list could go on, but the point that needs emphasizing is simply that, if God has arranged your circumstances so that both parents must work, ask God to lead you to a day care facility that will serve your child well. A carefully chosen day care can be a real advantage for your children and can be an instrument for good.

Security Blankets and Thumb Sucking

Young children are predisposed to get away with as much as possible at home. Most young children participate in some form of habitual behavior like blanket-dragging or thumb-sucking. Questions about these seemingly minor problems always come up in parenting workshops, and I assume it is on the mind of most parents with children in the younger age groups.

Many parents have asked what to do with a four-year-old who will be starting school soon, but continues to suck his thumb or need a blanket for security.

What's a mother to do? Nothing!

It is important to recognize that children are more sensitive

70

to the comments of their age-mates than their parents are. We know from experience that 99.9% of children with some form of habitual behavior give up the behavior within the first week or two of school.

The key is to resist the temptation to over-control and possibly do more harm than good by attempting to steal, hide, incinerate, bury or otherwise do away with the security blanket. With thumbsucking, the same principle applies. Rather than put mustard or fish oil on the magic thumb, ignore the behavior—knowing that the kids in the neighborhood and at school will not ignore it. Often the behavior stops without a single comment from parents.

If it doesn't stop after a few weeks, then counseling and behavioral treatments are available, but this is rarely needed. Parent power in this regard comes from letting the environment supply some negative reinforcement and by not being too controlling.

Discipline and Tantrums

The specifics of discipline are not of major importance with very young children, but the principle being taught is. We want to be very careful to let our children know who is in charge at home from the very beginning. We are not talking dictatorship, just obedience to the admonition from God to rule (manage) one's house well (I Timothy 3:4). Although directed specifically to pastors, elders and deacons, the principle applies clearly to every parent with the God-given responsibility of leadership within a family.

Usually it is ineffective to spank babies, but beginning with toddlers, discipline should become more significant as a teaching device. As the child moves through his early years, spanking should be less frequent at seven than at six, less at nine than at eight, and so on. It is not that the child grows out of the need for discipline, but rather the methods should change. We do not expect a five-year-old to have the same level of understanding as an eight-year-old, so why should the discipline remain unchanged?

What is important is that the child becomes aware of the parent's power in the home. Not oppressive power, but loving

71

and compassionate power that loves enough to say "no" and isn't afraid to make the hard choices of child-rearing which include effective, consistent discipline.

A child's temper tantrum is a battle for power. When it comes to tantrums and other forms of early power plays, the parent must recognize the motivation and exercise the proper amount of loving power to control the child. Tantrums have only one purpose—to gain the upper hand with a parent or other caregiver.

Tantrums in young children *never* happen when they are alone. Tantrum behavior is done to get an adult's attention or to divert the adult from doing what the child doesn't want done. The ability to handle tantrum behavior is not scarce or hard to develop, and there is an effective way to control such displays. We must be able to give oursleves permission to remove the child from the presence of others, place him in his room and say, "Do not kick the walls or injure the room or yourself. When you are finished, you can come out." Then close the door and walk away.

No child tantrums alone. This expression of parent power and control will, in a very short time, eliminate the tantrum behavior. If the child does kick the walls, a spanking or some other form of discipline is in order. If the child is hyperactive or emotionally unstable, other methods can be applied. It is also important to realize that if the child is older, isolation will not work as well. But for the young child who is otherwise normal, such an expression of parent power can be relied on to discourage the behavior from happening again.

Godly Influence and Parent Power Begin at Home

We begin at the beginning again, being reminded that we are the first gods our children know. If children are exposed to Christian parents who can express love *and* authority, they will develop a significant advantage as they grow. Children of parents who love but are unwilling or unable to control become frightened, sensing an unwillingness in the parent to fight for their safety and an inability to make the hard choices of parenting.

Young children exposed to powerful parents lacking in the ability to express love become abused children, alternately angry and hostile or withdrawn and depressed. Either extreme can destroy children and make it very difficult for them ever to grasp the love of a powerful God, a God who loved them enough to sacrifice His only Son and is powerful enough to forgive their sins. We do so much more than parent young children. We provide the foundation for their future relationship with God.

FOOTNOTES:
[1] Erickson, Eric, *Childhood and Society* ©1963, Norton Publishers, N.Y., N.Y.

5
POWER PARENTING THE SCHOOL-AGED CHILD

Judy Collins was heading off into her first day at kindergarten. Even though her mother had been on the verge of tears all morning, she was able to keep them from showing until the moment they walked into the classroom. As Judy let go of her mother's hand and walked through the door, her mom let go of the tears, trying hard not to let Judy see that she was crying.

On the way home that morning, Mrs. Collins thought about the preparation she and her husband had given Judy so she would not fight against leaving home and going to school today. They had talked to their daughter about the fun of school and all the things she would do, things they just couldn't do at home. They had even taken Judy for a walk around the school last spring to make it more familiar to her.

And it worked. Judy eased into her school career without a hint of tears, unlike her mother, and did not even turn around to wave goodbye as Mom left school.

Mrs. Collins wondered why she felt so bad about this new experience for her daughter. Judy would be coming home that afternoon, full of excitement and stories about her day and eager to tell her mom what it was like. Judy's mom knew everything was going to go well, so why was she still apprehensive about the first day of school?

Moving Out Slowly

Judy's mom gradually realized that what was bothering her was not the first day of school, but the realization that this day had permanently changed the relationship between Judy and her parents. This *was* the first step in a process that would

74

eventually end with Judy moving out of the home to go to college or to get married, and would mean that she was, in fact, on her own.

Mrs. Collins was upset with the prospect of gradual but irreversible power loss, a reduction in the influence she and her husband had worked so hard to develop with Judy. One that had, so far, produced very favorable results. Judy's mom was worried, way down deep inside, that maybe the school would counteract the moral and spiritual principles Judy had been raised to believe. All the teachers at the school seemed very nice, and Judy's teacher was very pleasant and apparently very knowledgeable about young children. But Mrs. Collins had heard so much about the problems of secular humanism being taught in the public schools, that she was concerned. She had even heard that religion was being left out of the newer textbooks. She worried if this would be true even for children in kindergarten.

Mrs. Collins was concerned about losing influence with her daughter, losing it to teachers and even to Judy's new school friends. She was concerned that years of effort could be lost to the six hours or so a day of school Judy would eventually experience. Perhaps the books she would read in later grades would not be acceptable, or maybe Judy would be ridiculed if she witnessed of her faith to the other kids. Maybe she would give in to peer pressure and actually reject the things her parents had taught her.

And it was only Judy's first day at school!

School Influence and Parent Influence

Yes, school does change children! No doubt about it. But after all, isn't that what we pay teachers and administrators to do? We don't want our children to stay the same as a result of their schooling! No, we expect change, but we want the change to be in the same general direction as the plan of life we have established for our children. We want them to acquire knowledge and the ability to use that knowledge, but we don't want them changed in regard to the deeper meanings of life, meanings *we* have instilled in them through their first five years at home.

We want change, and yet, we don't want change. We want education without indoctrination. And we want our children to grow up to believe what we have taught them, even if it is different from what the schools have taught. We want the school's influence to move children in the same direction as our influence has moved them, and to do so with as little controversy as possible. Schools are expected to do the job of educating while leaving the job of "raising" to the parents.

What Mrs. Collins will eventually realize is that a school, any school, will not change basic family values as long as they are *real* family values. Six or seven hours of school each day for about 180 days each year will not be sufficient to overwhelm the first years of parental teaching, what is taught to the growing child in the *other* eighteen hours in the day at home, and the *other* 185 days of the year when school in not in session.

But watch out for the void!

The only time a school will be influential in indoctrinating a child of any age is when that child is left with a void, a vacuum in some area of knowledge. Schools are generally not out to propagandize our children or to convince them that their parents' ideas are wrong. Teachers don't want that kind of trouble generally.

But, if our children are not properly taught by lesson or example at home, the school can be expected to step in and *fill that void* created by incomplete or inefficient parenting. Parent power and influence is not lost just because a child is enrolled in public school. Parent power and influence *will* be sacrificed to the void of missed moral lessons at home or imperfect modeling by parents. If Christian parents are careful about their parenting responsibilities under God and give sufficient attention to teaching and living the truths they consider important at home, a few hours of school each day *will not change that teaching!*

Our three children have attended Christian schools from kindergarten through high school. We have always been thankful that God allowed us to act on our convictions about the value of Christian education for our children. But we also recognize that other Christian parents may not have those same convictions, and we would not criticize those who choose public schools for their children.

There was a time when, because of a move to a new area, our oldest child attended a public junior high school for a year. In the course of the year, we experienced the normal kinds of controversies about evolution, ultimate values, situational ethics, and so on. We also found that we could depend on our teenager to give *us* the benefit of the doubt when confronted in the classroom about religion, evolution, or values.

Linda and I were greatly comforted by the realization that our child placed our opinions and values above those of others. Yes, our teenager heard all the evolutionary teachings, and while she undoubtedly learned something about the fabled dinosaurs and cave-dwellers, when she balanced the new information against that which she had been exposed to all the previous years of teaching both in the school and at home, Darwin didn't stand a chance.

I can't blame Mrs. Collins for being concerned about Judy's school experiences. But if Judy continues to be raised in a God-honoring home by parents who are not afraid to confront the difficult issues of modern Christian living, Judy's school will only reinforce what she has been taught at home.

Healthy Christian Families

Dr. Paul Meier is a Christian psychiatrist connected with Dallas Theological Seminary and the Minirth and Meier Clinic. Dr. Meier has written an excellent book on Christian parenting from the perspective of a Christian parent *and* a Christian psychiatrist. In his book, *Christian Child-Rearing and Personality Development,*[1] he identifies five factors found in mentally healthy Christian families. These five factors are derived from years of work with Christian families needing some degree of psychiatric or counseling help. They will help to illustrate how we can maintain our power and influence with our children, even when they attend public school.

Factor #1: Love

Dr. Meier emphasizes the great importance of love in healthy families, but he goes beyond the normal sentimental idea of love. Love must be felt by and expressed to children if they are to grow up mentally and spiritually healthy. It is one thing to love our children, but it can be quite something else to actually *express* the love.

No one needs to be reminded of that love more than the school-aged child going face to face with the cold realities of the world every day. Our children are going to realize that there are actually kids in school who don't particularly like them and who won't put up with the behaviors they have gotten away with at home. Leaving the warmth of home each morning requires a healthy dose of "love reminder" from Mom and Dad along with the ham sandwich and apple.

When love is felt and honestly expressed in the home, the child is equipped with a form of emotional armor that is nearly invincible. If there are chinks in that armor such as poor parental modeling, inconsistent discipline, or favoritism, they will show up in a variety of weaknesses and stress reactions in elementary school children. Love is security to children, and love provides them with a reason for obeying parents and for maintaining the values they learned at home.

A father once told me, "I don't have to tell my children I love them. I come home every night with food for the table, don't I?"

Wrong!

Children might not need daily reaffirmations of their parents' love for them, but sincere reminders can only strengthen them.

It is also important that children see love exprssed between parents. I am not talking about leaving the bedroom door open, as some have suggested. But a normal hug and kiss type behavior will let the kids know that Mom and Dad are still in love (as corny as that may seem to children) and that their *security* is not threatened. Remember, security is a basic need of children of all ages. A simple expression of love between

Mom and Dad will reinforce their confidence that they are not at risk to become divorce statistics as has happened to nearly 50% of other kids at school.

A healthy Christian family needs vertical love (parent to child) and horizontal love (parent to parent) to withstand the tendency to feel unloved and uncared for while at school.

Factor #2: Discipline

Discipline is "in" again. Even the most liberal writers and educators are in favor of discipline these days, although the definition of discipline will vary from expert to expert and almost never includes physical methods. Discipline has regained some of its former power and importance because of the failure of liberal and permissive methods during the sixties and seventies in America. Children raised during these times are now parents themselves and have rejected the permissive style of parenting in favor of a more conservative tone.

Dr. Meier includes discipline for many reasons, not the least of which is that discipline serves as a reminder of love for children. We discussed this in an earlier chapter, and we will examine discipline thoroughly later in this book. For now, though, let's realize again that while many things send the message, "I love you" to children, nothing does it better than a clear, compassionate, and reasonable system of family discipline.

There is another kind of discipline important for the health of families, too. *Self-discipline* on the part of parents sends a strong message to children that self-control is expected and is a standard in the home. Parents who smoke or drink will have obvious and serious difficulties with children who want to do the same things when they get to be teenagers. "That's no problem in our house," you may say, but before we get self-righteous about not smoking or using alcohol, how about over-eating?

Many good Christian parents who would not dream of hurting their testimonies—or their bodies—by using tobacco or alcohol, don't give a second thought about the damaged testimony brought on by being fifty pounds overweight. Discipline comes in many shapes and colors. Abstaining from harmful substances is only one of many ways to show Christ's control in a life.

Factor #3: Consistency

School-aged children can tolerate almost anything but inconsistency. When parents behave in an unpredictable manner toward their children, the confusion and fear that result can last a lifetime.

Consistency is a sign of both mental and emotional stability in parents and a prime characteristic of a well-run family. Parental consistency is shown through daily behaviors rather than special events. Consistency is shown in the way parents conduct their public and private lives, and consistency shows up in the way children grow and adjust to the demands of the world.

Unfortunately, there are several common forms of parental inconsistency found in Christian families.

I have dealt with parents who professed to be Christians but who were unwilling or unable to stop using tobacco or alcohol. Smoking is a particular problem in the southeast and especially in those states where tobacco has a long tradition. I have counseled with Christian parents who came to me for suggestions on how to stop a teenager from smoking when one or both parents were habitual smokers. I have counseled with Christian parents who claimed to be only "social" drinkers but who were concerned that their teenager might be experimenting with marijuana.

Inconsistency is a destructive force in the life of a family. Inconsistency tells children and teenagers that Mom and Dad lack the character, intelligence, or strength needed to lead a family, or that they lack sufficient love for the children. *Surely,* the reasoning goes, *if Mom and Dad really cared for me, they would see how scary their inconsistency is to me.* Inconsistency not only threatens the family unit, but is also a prime factor in adolescent and childhood mental breakdowns and depression. Psychologists call this kind of parent

80

behavior "double-bind," and research has proven that children and teenagers cannot tolerate a double-bind type of parenting for very long.

Factor #4: Modeling

What we are is more important to our children than what we say or do.

Jesus emphasized the importance of modeling when He was training His disciples, and He continued to emphasize it throughout His ministry on earth. Parents can benefit by this emphasis, and be encouraged to recognize the power of modeling, considering what kind of models we are for our children.

A father can live and die, never uttering a word of how much love he has for his children, and the children will always know whether or not they were loved. A mother can raise ten children, never verbalizing with them the feeling of confidence she has in them, and they will always know how much they were trusted. While it is true that we don't *have* to tell our children how much we love and trust them, we should do it anyway.

The point is obvious, though. Our behavior so far overshadows our words that they are not even in the same league. We can't fool our kids. Children, even the very young, sense inconsistency in behavior or words and react accordingly. We are models for our children even if separated by death or divorce. Boys learn to be men and husbands from their fathers. Girls learn to be women and wives from their mothers. They learn these things not by listening, but by watching.

Factor #5: A man at the head of the family

This one would get a lot of liberals excited. Dr. Meier states in very definite terms that healthy families are led by two parents, one of whom accepts responsibility under God for the leadership of the family unit. He emphasizes the shared power of mother and father but recognizes that God has ordained the husband and father to take leadership in spiritual matters.

Even though this principle has often been abused by fathers who have only a partial knowledge of what the Bible says about the ideal Christian family, the occasional abuse in no way affects the truth of the principle of godly leadership.

Father-led families are more likely to be healthy families because they are stronger. Two parents are not only better than one, they are stronger than one, especially when each parent understands and obeys what God expects (Ecclesiastes 4:9-12). Father-led families are what God intended. As the world moves farther and farther from this model, we will see more families breaking up and more children suffering because of the behavior of their parents.

Industry or Inferiorty: Self-Concept and School

Erik Erikson, the developmental theorist, suggested eight separate and distinct stages of development throughout life. At each stage the person is faced with a decision point, a fork in the road of life leading in two opposite directions. One road leads to health and good development, the other to maladjustment and slowed development. Erikson's name for the stage of life experienced by the elementary school child is "Industry versus Inferiority."

Erikson's idea has shown itself to be true in large measure. He believes school aged children face the choice of becoming industrious and capable or incompetent and inferior. His theory states that elementary school children are supposed to acquire a sense of being able to tackle any job in the belief that he or she stands a reasonable chance of succeeding at it. Erikson holds that school children are to learn attitude before facts, a sense of competence before specific skills.

The challenge for school children in the early grades, especially, is to acquire a positive attitude toward school in general. We want our kids to come out of the first few grades believing they can learn anything placed before them; then they can do whatever the teacher asks. Usually, schools do not give quantitative grades in the first three years. Report cards are filled with teacher comments and recommendations

82

instead. Elementary school teachers are charged with the task of teaching skills, such as reading and math, within a pleasant and reinforcing classroom.

School *is supposed* to be fun for the younger kids, and if it isn't, major problems will surface. A school that is fun is filled with rewards for doing well. Not money or candy, of course, but teacher praise and happy-faced papers sent home will make parents smile, too. A school is also a place of learning where younger children can succeed at their own level, a necessary requirement because of the differing rates of maturation in young children.

If school is not a fun place to be, children begin the process of convincing themselves that they do not belong there because no child will voluntarily stay where he feels unwanted or incompetent. If a child is not learning because of a learning disability, visual impairment, or poor home conditions, the school becomes an "aversive stimulus" causing anxiety and fear in place of optimism and fun.

Children who experience school as a good place to be can be expected to develop what Erikson called a "sense of industry," a state of mind leading to a willingness to take on any challenge, problem, or task in the full belief that they have a reasonable chance of succeeding. These children get good grades because they expect to do well, and 99% of what happens in elementary school is attitude-based.

Children who experience school as a bad and unpleasant place learn to hate what schools stand for—failure and incompetence. When school isn't fun for a child, absences increase, grades drop, and the self-fulfilling prophecy begins, virtually assuring the continued failure and eventual withdrawal of these children. They have found the road to inferiority, and sadly, there are very few exit ramps on this highway.

For Christian parents as well as other parents, knowledge is power. Knowing what to expect from our elementary school is important because it has been so long since parents were there. Some Christian schools are rigid, stark, and un-fun even in the early grades. I have spoken with graduates of many Christian schools who did *not* enjoy their early school experience, and, while in college now, are still struggling with their feelings of incompetence and the desire to get away from education. Of course, the overwhelming majority of public and private elementary schools are as they should be: fun, exciting, and rewarding.

Developmental Milestones

What kind of changes should parents expect to see in the years between kindergarten and junior high school? It is easy to see the physical growth taking place and the new skills and abilities putting in their appearance. But what about internal changes, the kind that are not so easy to see?

Internal changes in thought and personality always show up in the behavior of children, and it should be possible for parents to look at the observable behaviors and know what is happening inside. What follows is a fairly comprehensive listing of these developmental milestones as they appear in normal children.

Quasi-Adult thought

During the elementary school years, children normally move into the domain of adult thought and language. This is a gradual process producing relatively small changes at first, but the changes are cumulative, piling one on top of the other until the differences from year to year are very noticeable and impressive.

Limitations on the thoughts of the school-aged child focus primarily on language abilities, particularly vocabulary. It is extremely important that parents use proper language around their children. Not only moral and non-offensive language, but your speech should employ words the child can understand and think about *and* which will include a few words that the child does not know but will ask about. We need to help our children exercise their thought and language abilities, and, at the same time, encourage them to stretch themselves by learning new words.

Christian parents have an extra responsibility to create as many protections as possible for their children in the area of thought and language. We exhibit our God-given power and influence with our children by setting the right kind of example in all forms of our adult behavior, including language, in preparation for the day our children will enter the real world without us. How we talk reflects clearly how we think; our children will imitate both.

Conscience and Morality

There is no neutrality when it comes to human beings. As long as people, and not robots are involved, neutrality will remain a myth. Values are as normal a part of human growth and development as inches and pounds—and are much more important.

Moral children and young people grow from the seed-bed of prepared Christian parenting. As certainly as there is an "age of responsibility" for children, there is a lifetime of responsibility for parents who cannot help but influence their children in one direction or another. Conscience and morality are imitative behaviors in children, a reflection of what they have seen and heard at home.

During the elementary school years, we expect our children to learn the morality of sharing, cooperation, helping, and protecting those weaker than themselves. We expect our children to learn (hopefully from us!) the value of honesty and humility when dealing with others. School aged children are expected to obey the rules without serious complaints and respect the authority of parents, teachers, and other adults. In other words, we want our children to begin the process of becoming civilized, as we discussed earlier, and to show an honest appreciation for the values they learned at home.

A lot happens in the area of morality during these years, but it all revolves around the basic fact that our children imitate and reflect the morality, values, and sense of conscience they learned at home. In this area, children will do what they have seen done at home.

Socialization

Social cooperation is easier said than done, as any recess supervisor can verify. But it is precisely that skill which is acquired in part or in whole from the school experience. We send our kids to school with personality, intelligence, and character, but it remains to be seen how they will apply these principles when the sneaker hits the playground. Social experiences in both structured and unstructured activities become the base from which more adult behaviors may grow.

Another important part of this process is self-evaluation. The ability to correctly gauge one's abilities in relation to playmates is crucial in good self-concept formation. Home education has some advantages, but one overwhelming disadvantage is the inability to adequately interrelate with others of the same age. It takes many interactions with many different children before we begin to become realistic about our abilities and limitations; a few neighbor children will not be enough for most kids.

Socialization is a term that gets knee-jerk reactions from some Christians, but call it what you will, the process of learning to deal with age-mates is an indispensable part of growing up well.

Physical development

In most children growth is slow and steady until puberty strikes, and growth spurts are experienced. Elementary school aged children gain about 2 ½ inches and 3 to 6 pounds per year under normal circumstances. Their physical appearance becomes more adult-like, and they improve in running, jumping, coordination, throwing, catching, and balancing. Most children within this age group are active and experience progressively improved reactions with matching growth in gross and fine motor skills.

It is not the normally developing child that is of concern, of course, but we will look at a full discussion of growth abnormalities and special problems in a later chapter. It is however, important for parents to recognize the relatively wide range of "normal" when discussing children and to become tolerant of children who do not quite match up to our expectations as yet. Significant damage has been done by parents who stressed physical attributes to the exclusion of intellectual and moral abilities only to pay the heavy price of rejection later.

Self-Concept Development

Self-concept in children is created by parents. Each child possesses a basic sense of self prior to entering school, a sense developed by interacting with parents and other family members and by making comparisons of self with family and neighbor children.

At the time a child enters school, his self-concept is in for some re-organization. Experiences at school confirm or contradict what the child has learned at home about the kind of a kid he or she is. Interactions with teachers and classmates slowly become major contributors to the self-concept that was begun at home.

Self-concept stems from five parts of the self. These five components, taken together, tell children what to think about themselves. These elements may not overwhelm what was instilled at home, but they do serve to strengthen or weaken areas of self-concept.

Academic Self-Concept

The academic part of a child's self-concept depends on the level of agreement between how the child expects to do in school and what he or she actually does. To what extent do grades match expectations?

There is a very important point to be made about having reasonable expectations for our children in school. It may sound nice to say we expect only A's and B's from our children, but for those children who cannot earn high grades, this optimism in parents can be the most tragic and unpleasant facet of the child's school experience. The key is to have *and to communicate* reasonable expectations to our children. Otherwise we induce stresses that may not be able to be resolved within the child. We want them to do *their best*, and we want to accept those honest attempts at doing their best.

87

I have counseled with straight A students who had lousy academic self-concepts, and I have counseled with low C students who loved school and wouldn't miss a day of it. Academic self-concept is based on *the amount of agreement between what is expected and what is achieved!* It is not based on high grades alone. To be sure, most children with high grades will have good academic self-concepts simply because they have been successful in school. But some children are unable to attain high grades all the way through school.

Educational experts tell us that most people today are not able to do academic work at a level needed to graduate from college. Christian parents seem to have special difficulty dealing with this fact, believing that college is simply taken for granted if the motivation is there. This idea is obviously not true. We are going to sacrifice some of our God-given power and influence with our adult children if we insist that they "should" be able to do academic work *they* know is beyond them. College is not for everyone, a fact that is equally true for Christians as for non-Christians.

Social Self-Concept

School and the family are the primary socialization agents in present-day America. For those of us who attend church regularly, this becomes a third important force in the process.

Social self-concept is based on the child's ideal self as compared to the self he or she sees in the eyes of friends and family members. The ideal self is a glorified and usually unrealistic idea of what we would like to be like if we could wish ourselves different. Ideal self is what children and teenagers dream about: the beautiful, popular, intelligent, and heavily sought after girl, or the tall, muscular, smart, and super athletic boy. Ideal self begins very early in life and never goes away, although it becomes less powerful when, as we become adults, we realize our limitations.

The word for this is *congruence*, and it means the level of agreement between ideal self and real self. A child's social self-concept depends on the level of congruence between what is and what is hoped for. Social self-concept is based on the behavior of others as each of us interacts with our friends and associates. Social self-concept never stops changing because we never stop growing.

With whom do your children compare themselves?

Rambo?

Cartoon characters on television?

The other kids in school and in the neighborhood?

We strengthen our children when we provide a large group of children with whom they can grow. Wise Christian parents will choose a school carefully, recognizing the school as a tool in the civilization of their children. This is one of the major arguments in the debate over whether public or Christian schools are best for the children of Christian parents. Regardless of personal feelings on that issue, it is important to provide opportunities for comparison and self-evaluation which lead to a good *and* accurate social self-concept.

Spiritual Self-Concept

Moral standards are *always* communicated to children, even by parents who claim no particular religion or philosophic creed. The absence of belief is a statement about the irrelevance of belief. The belief in a moral standard is a statement about those who do not hold such a standard.

Because it is impossible to raise children to be neutral on moral or religious issues, we recognize that each child will develop a spiritual sense of self just as he or she did with academics and friends.

Spiritual self-concept is based on the level of agreement, or congruence, between what is "good" and what the child actually does. If a child or young person acts in accordance with what is believed to be good behavior, that child can be expected to have a satisfactory spiritual self-concept. A child who behaves outside what is held to be acceptable may have a lot of fun, but the spiritual component of self-concept will be low.

Often we find the Holy Spirit using this disagreement between what should be done and what is done to bring a person to the point of conviction about his relationship with Christ. An imbalanced spiritual self-concept should not, however, be seen as a problem in children because perfect children, as perfect adults, do not feel the need of a Saviour. Children, much more than adults, are in the process of becoming, and we need to resist the temptation to expect completeness too soon.

Psychological Self-Concept

The first chapter of James warns that "a double-minded man is unstable in all his ways" (James 1:8). Any person can become double-minded and thus unstable. This happens when one believes, yet doubts, or cannot make up his mind.

Children should be expected to be double-minded. They are in the process of forming their own ideas about things and simply have not made any conclusions yet on a whole host of important issues. The process of becoming single-minded is a developmental one that culminates sometime in adulthood, but never in childhood.

A well-balanced psychological self-concept is a goal of good child-rearing rather than an experience of good child-rearing. The process of making up one's mind on important issues must be allowed to proceed slowly in children. Hurrying this process frequently results in a legalistic and often temporary answer to very complex questions. We can be content to wait for our kids to come to the correct answers, the answers we are living in front of them day by day. Or, we can let our insecurity and impatience force them to hurry along this path and thereby miss the reasons for the answers they have been given.

Power in Christian parenting is trusting the Holy Spirit to lead our children along the correct path at the correct speed, giving all the right lessons time to sink in and not hurrying them past important forks in the road.

Physical Self-Concept

God plays no favorites. The nose you were given or the feet I have are there for a purpose, even if we must wait for death or the rapture to find out what the purpose was.

Our children will not be all we want them to be physically. More importantly, they will not be all *they* want to be either. But as we live our Christianity in front of them every day, our attitudes about the bodies and health God gave us will influence how they feel about their bodies.

We can help our children's physical self-concept by demonstrating a healthy appreciation for God's goodness to us in giving us the health and the body we have. Grouching and complaining about being overweight or underweight, about having too little hair or too much nose, just gives kids permission to start criticizing God on their own for the imperfect body they live inside.

We can also help our children develop a healthy physical self-concept by emphasizing that sexual divisions are God-given. After all, God could have created five sexes instead of two, but He made two and gave one *spiritual* authority over the other. Throughout the New Testament and, especially, in the book of Galatians, we are told repeatedly that God values each of us and planned the sex of the body we inhabit for our good and His honor (I Timothy 6:17; Galatians 3:26-28).

God plays no favorites and He *does* have a sense of humor—just look at the varieties of bodies He has created. A healthy attitude about *our* adult bodies will help our children develop proper physical self-concepts.

School Based Concerns
Dealing with teachers

Having been a public school teacher for seven years prior to moving to college level teaching, I am convinced that the great majority of teachers in every kind of school see parents as allies, not enemies. Teachers know their job is impossible without the support of parents, and schools place great emphasis on encouraging teachers to build bridges with parents for the benefit of the children.

When there is a disciplinary matter to be dealt with, parents should accept the judgment of the teacher as the final word and avoid taking sides with their child against the teacher. Parents can be advocates for their children in the school system without modeling an anti-school, anti-authority attitude that will backfire eventually. If an adult in the school claims that my child was seen doing something wrong, I will accept that word over my child's denial under normal circumstances. If a teacher says that another child saw my child do something and is the only witness, and my child denies doing it, I will believe my child every time.

Teachers have a right to be treated like honest adults in the school setting and when this kind of respect is forthcoming from parents, teachers will usually respond with at least an equal amount of respect for the wishes and concerns of parents. I will be my child's advocate at every opportunity, but I do not want to model an un-Christian attitude of attacking legitimate authority just to let my child know I am on his side. If parents are on their children's side, they will know it by the general attitude and actions displayed in other areas of family life.

Under-achievement

No challenge is greater for parents than trying to know the level of schoolwork appropriate for a child. Under-achievement is a major problem for parents primarily because often we don't know what our kids are capable of doing, especially in the elementary grades.

Any school will have testing facilities so that a child doing poorly in his classes can be tested to see if the problem is one of motivation, intelligence, or a special problem such as a learning disability. The key for parents who want to remain powerful in the child's elementary school experience is to get this kind of evaluation done as soon as the problem shows itself. The testing service is one of the things our taxes pay for, and we shouldn't be reluctant to ask the school to provide them.

If under-achievement is identified as intelligence-related or caused by a learning disability, special arrangements can be made by the school to provide the special classes and attention the child needs. If under-achievement is attributed to motivation, then parents should sit down with the school counselor, discuss the problem and what to do about it.

Elementary counselors and school psychologists are specially trained to deal with these difficulties and should be seen as friends and allies of the family in helping a child.

Hyperactivity

Hyperactivity is so common in elementary school children that it deserves special consideration on its own.

Experts estimate that about 10% of elementary school children are hyperactive. This condition, which falls under the heading of a learning disability, is more common in younger children and gradually diminishes (for presently unknown reasons) so that nearly all children have outgrown it by adolescence.

The challenge for parents is to recognize the problem as soon as possible and make the necessary changes in the child's diet and environment. Make a visit to the pediatrician to see if medical treatment is appropriate and then pray for tolerance and patience.

One of our three children was hyperactive. She grew out of the hyperactivity by about thirteen or so, but is was a month-by-month battle with school personnel to help them understand that her fidgety misbehavior and difficulty in paying attention in class were not of her making. Medicine helped a great deal, of course, and the problem slowly lessened, eventually disappearing completely. We were able to prevent academic damage from occurring, but it was not easy.

You can expect the hyperactive child to have difficulty in behavior because of the impulsive, quick-to-act nature of hyperactivity. These kids will have trouble with age-mates because their fidgety behavior bothers the other kids and makes them unpopular with their age-mates. Their grades will suffer because of the short attention span and distractability. Many of these kids also become emotional basketcases because they feel guilty as a result of always being in trouble at school *and* at home.

You stand a better chance of having a hyperactive child to raise than any other kind of problem child. We wrestled with this issue for many years until learning that God gives us the children who need *us,* not vice versa. If you are the parent of a hyperactive child, you can raise that child successfully, but you will need generous amounts of patience and tolerance. You will also need to become educated on the subject.

God doesn't expect parents to surrender their power and influence with a child He has given them simply because the child is more difficult to raise than some others. Difficult children *can* be reared in a God-honoring way, with success, if we realize where we get the strength to do the job.

Childhood suicide

According to the U.S. government, approximately one in every 100,000 10-14 year olds will commit suicide. The statistic goes up to nine per 100,000 in the 15-19 year old group. The rate is not declining. Most suicides in young people happen during adolescence, but even one child or pre-teen turning to suicide is cause for great concern.

The reasons children and pre-teens attempt to commit suicide revolve primarily around their family situations. Since the family is the primary reference group for elementary school children, it is no surprise that when the family breaks up, Mom or Dad dies, or some other crisis comes along that threatens the basic security of children, some will seek a desperate escape. Although it is true that children will sometimes attempt to manipulate their parents by threatening or attempting a form of suicide.

The notes suicidal children write tell of feeling unloved and unwanted, a state of mind one writer believes led to the idea of "throwaway kids." Filled with rejection and despair, feeling expendable is the common denominator. We find abused children account for about 40% of suicide attempts.

We will examine suicide in detail in the chapter on adolescence, but for now we can look at some common suicide warning signs in children.

Remember that children are not as sophisticated as teenagers in hiding their feelings, so we can expect to find outright statements of what the child is considering doing. They are often phrased in terms of just asking for help to escape stress. Sudden changes in behavior often precede a suicide attempt, as does a gradual move to being moody and apathetic, not enjoying anything anymore. Children contemplating suicide tend to have problems sleeping and eating normally; they will probably start missing school with undefined illnesses, just "feeling bad" in the morning.

What should a parent do when these signs appear?

Get help!

The overwhelming majority of suicidal kids can be helped, but they will never get better if the problem is ignored in hopes that it will just "go away." Check with the child guidance clinic in your area; talk to your pediatrician, or, if need be, take the child to a hospital emergency room. Almost every hospital with an emergency room has facilities and personnel to handle psychiatric emergencies.

We should never ignore a problem like this in hopes of it just going away. Too many parents have lost children because they would not face the reality of having a disturbed and unhappy child.

There is much required of parents who really want to be the best parents possible. Sometimes it feels like it just can't be done, especially with more than one child in elementary school at the same time. But God is still able, and He expects us to continue to be an influence for good in the lives of our children even when they move slowly away from us into the educational and social world. Remember, God said that to whom much is given, much shall be required (Luke 12:48). But the same God who said that, also said, "My grace is sufficient for thee" (II Corinthians 12:9).

Prepared parents remain powerful and influential parents throughout the lives of their children, even grown children. The influence changes, of course, but the impact of our parenting remains *if* we know what we are doing and meet God's requirements to be the kind of spiritual leaders our children need.

Knowledge is power, and God would have none of us to be ignorant.

FOOTNOTES:
[1] Meier, Paul, *Christian Child-Rearing and Personality Development* © 1977, Baker Book House, Grand Rapids, Michigan.

6
POWER PARENTING
IN THE "TWEEN YEARS"

Alex—The Awkward Brain

The years between childhood and adulthood are not easy for anyone, but they seemed especially hard on Alex, a thirteen-year-old I met about a year ago. Alex was trying hard to become a teenager, but he wasn't having much success. His problem was that his brain had become a teenager before his body. While he was a real whiz kid in school subjects, he felt miserably unpopular because of his gangly appearance, the pimples beginning to sprout on his forehead, and the fact that he always seemed to say the wrong thing at the wrong time.

And girls! Alex just hung his head in dejection when *that* subject came up. Alex could tell me the ins and outs of the hypotenuse triangle and how a laser works, but he didn't know how to talk to a girl or how to keep from laughing at the wrong time when the other boys were telling jokes on the teacher. Alex wanted to know why he could be so smart in school and be so miserable every place else, and why teachers seemed to like him more than the other kids—a questionable blessing under the best of circumstances.

As we talked, it became clear that Alex was experiencing some depression over his situation. He was genuinely upset and wanted some answers.

Was he going to stay this way, so awkward and uncomfortable?

Was he ever going to look like the older boys? The ones in high school with the cars and lots of friends?

Would he ever be able to talk to a girl without falling apart?

Alex needed some answers!

When Puberty Strikes

Alex was upset because of the changes brought on by puberty, a normal stage in development that bridges the gap between childhood and adulthood. There are many ways to define this event, but it is generally agreed to be the time when the testes and prostate gland, or the uterus and vagina, mature and enlarge preparing the body for reproduction.

These changes are accompanied by alterations in appearance, as Alex was unhappily experiencing, including growth in general body shape and size along with gradual changes in the relative proportions of muscle, fat, and bone. In addition to the sex-related changes, appearance factors related to sexual identity develop.

Younger adolescents also experience facial changes. The forehead becomes more prominent, both jaws grow forward (in anticipation of orthodontics), the chin becomes more pointed, and facial muscles develop along with a decrease in the fat layer just under the surface of the skin.

All these changes and more afflict "tween-agers" and create the need for some serious parental understanding. Parents are prone to smile at the unusual appearance and spidery-legged awkwardness in young adolescents, but the kids aren't smiling. They are mortified!

What our kids need from us is calm reassurance that they will grow through these changes and will eventually get a body that is closer to expectations than the one they currently inhabit. We need to remember that all teenagers have an idea of what they "should" look like, an *ideal self* that is a composite of their dreams and experiences, the movies and television shows they have seen, and the older kids they know. They are sensitive to body image stereotypes of what a fat or skinny kid should be like, or what to expect from a slow-developing kid or one who gets an adult body early.

Every teenager of any age is unhappy with his or her body. Talk to an adolescent about how he looks and everyone will know instantly what needs to be changed and what he is self-conscious about. It is simply the nature of the adolescent to be unhappy and self-conscious about his appearance, no matter how good he or she looks to others.

The sexual changes that occur need to be addressed by parents. There is probably no area so absent of parent power and influence in Christian families than sexual information. We tend to reject calls for sex education in the schools, but most of us will not bite the bullet and do the father/son or mother/daughter talk about sex. We need to help younger adolescents understand the biological processes behind menstruation and sexual thoughts, how to control the new sexual urges they are experiencing, and what to watch out for. Younger teenagers need reassurance that they aren't becoming perverts or monsters and that they need to give themselves time to adjust to the new body and new sexual nature they are experiencing.

Power parenting in this area is evidenced by parents not letting their adolescents drift free and blow in the winds of sexual ignorance. We express our love and concern for kids at this young age by telling them what they need to know and by giving them permission to hold off on sexual behavior until they catch up with their body.

Growth Abnormalities

The problem with puberty is that it is not a smooth process. Rather it comes in fits and starts like an old car getting cranked up for the first time in a long time. This was a major part of Alex's problem. Puberty produces physical and sexual changes that, under normal circumstances, will produce an acceptable end result, but the tween-ager has to learn to live with what comes before that end result.

Parents can help by knowing that while about 80% of young adolescents grow at about the same rate, the other 20% can be afflicted with one of four variations of abnormal growth patterns. If a teen with one of these variations is to have a happy life prior to full adolescence, parents must provide some understanding and love in the process.

The four differences in the growth pattern include early maturing girls, early maturing boys, late maturing girls, and late maturing boys. We are discussing physical maturity, not moral or psychological maturity. The question parents need to ask themselves is, "If one of my kids experiences one of these growth abnormalities, how can I help?" We also need to think about the unique problems and concerns of each of the four variations.

It is generally agreed that late maturing boys have the greatest burden. This is a boy who is the smallest in his class, the last one chosen for team games, the one likely to be picked on by bigger boys, and the one who is called "shrimp" by the girls. Not an easy load for a thirteen-or fourteen-year-old to carry.

Late maturing boys tend to have doubts about their sexuality, about their physical abilities, and their general self-concept. (Alex was *always* the last boy chosen for school teams). Late maturing boys need parents who are sensitive to their feelings of inferiority and who can reinforce good qualities with compliments. Late maturing boys can benefit from organized activities like Boy Scouts and camping opportunities where they can find things that they can do well, things that would have remained undiscovered at home.

Late maturing boys also need reassurance from Dad that he, too, was a late grower (this is almost always true) and that things will be okay down the road if he is patient. Boys afflicted with slow growth can do very well if the family is sensitive and strong.

Late maturing girls have a much lighter burden to carry than their male counterparts. Smallish girls are often thought of as "cute" by the other kids whereas smallish boys are just "shrimps." Late maturing girls will often do well in school, participate in the activities and sports for girls (which are usually less size oriented), and be given attention by older boys.

These girls will likely have some doubts about their sexuality as well, given that the beginning of menstruation is often delayed along with their growth. This frequently produces a feeling of still being a little girl instead of a young teenager. A sensitive mother can help with these uncertainties by sharing her experiences in going through this time in her life and how she dealt with her concerns. A strong family covers a multitude of uncertainties. Your teenagers need your strength.

Early maturing girls have another kind of problem to handle, one that has greater potential for life-changing difficulties. Girls who grow into women while still in their early teens are often envied by girls developing at a more normal rate, but any advantages to looking older are often outweighed by the temptations that go along with the more mature appearance.

Teachers and parents tend to treat the early maturing girl as the young adult she resembles, and the additional responsibility and respect often encourages the development of good traits of character and morality. The tragedy is that so many of these young adolescents fall to the temptations placed before them. They receive attention from older boys, boys with cars and opportunities to go places most thirteen-and fourteen-year-old girls normally cannot go. They can associate with an older crowd perhaps already into behaviors that are far beyond the ability of young teenage girls to deal with appropriately.

The answer to the biological and genetic occurrence of growing up fast lies in the family. The great majority of girls in the early maturing category deal well with their self-concept and the attention from older kids. A strong family that has taught moral values with love and consistency and modeled responsible decision-making for their daughter is not likely to face the negative impacts of early development. Parent power and godly influence are the keys to helping a fast-growing daughter survive and benefit from the experience of looking older.

There are very few negatives in the early development of boys. Early maturing boys have significant advantages over late maturing and normal boys. It is the early maturers who gain the physical skills in athletics first, along with the size and muscle to deter almost any challenger. Early maturing boys are chosen as leaders, both in school and out. They are thought of as being most likely to succeed by their teachers, have fewer problems with parental authority in the home, and are more likely to wind up as our astronauts, business and political leaders, and professional athletes.

There are some serious drawbacks under very negative environmental circumstances. In these circumstances, such boys can drift into or be forced into gangs and other forms of criminal activity for the same reasons their counterparts in positive environments become leaders of the football and debate teams. Poverty can turn the normal advantages of size and strength into disadvantages and may corrupt a potential business leader into a leader of illegal activity. Unfortunately, the one factor that would almost likely keep such a boy straight is often missing—a strong father.

Whichever alternative growth pattern your children experience, help is as near as your comments about your own growth history and how God never gives us more that we can bear—even if it means being the smallest boy in the seventh grade.

Children Becoming Young Adults

What parents see as they observe their younger teenagers begin the process of maturing to adulthood is not adolescence, but young adulthood. The term "adolescence" was created by western cultures around the turn of this century to help deal with the newly unneeded labor of America's youth. "Tweens" should be viewed as people in the earliest stages of adulthood rather than children in the last stages of childhood.

So, as we examine the changes that begin in the early teen years, let me emphasize again the importance of understanding this transition as one from child to adult, not childhood to adolescence and *then* adulthood. This is a point we will develop more fully in the next chapter, but the concept begins to be important now. With this in mind, we can look at the many life areas that undergo changes in the years between puberty and adulthood. We recognize that these changes are not complete until adulthood is fully realized, but I believe we can better understand the magnitude of the development our

101

kids experience if we can see the whole picture.

General social maturity

Peer relationships are the concern here. The "tweener" shows a lot of uncertainty about how to deal with friends and acquaintances, feeling socially awkward like Alex, and prone to slavish and uncontrollable imitations of age-mates. The difficulties of social insecurity are handled by most young teenagers by becoming carbon copies of one-another, thereby lessening the chances of being ridiculed or rejected.

The young adult handles social issues with a great deal more maturity and responsibility, to say nothing of being much more secure and self-confident. Social poise is more prevalent as is a greater resistance to both peer pressure and fad pressure. In fact, one of the primary ways maturity and adulthood is measured is by the individual's gradually becoming less faddish in clothing, hair, and behavior.

General emotional maturity

Young adolescents have trouble expressing their emotions in a socially acceptable and harmless way. I taught middle and junior high school for seven years, and I have never seen the degree of emotional explosiveness, giddy silliness, and emotional ups and downs as with young teens. These kids tend to handle problems by avoiding them if possible, and, if not possible, to lie about it. Events are seen as conspiring against them, and everything takes on an emotional color that defies rational explanation.

Young teenagers have a lot of trouble dealing with their emotions!

Young adults are another story. We grow to be able to handle negative emotions harmlessly and positive emotions acceptably. Young adults become much more objective and non-emotional in their interpretation of events and people. They tend to work to solve problems rather than to avoid them. There are fewer emotional hills and valleys in young adults, with a generally more serious attitude developing.

Heterosexual Interests

Elementary school-aged youngsters have very little interest

102

in the opposite sex. However, exclusive friendships with other members of one's own sex gradually give way to acute awareness of personal sexual changes, culminating in sparks of interest which usually begin around seventh grade for most kids.

The situation for the young adult bears no resemblance to the young teenager, of course. The difference shown most dramatically is the beginning of mate selection through extensive dating experiences. Young adults normally show a much more relaxed attitude about their sexuality with less need to "show-off" with clothing, muscle T-shirts, and stories of sexual conquests.

Movement is from virtually no interest to preoccupation with sexual matters. Although many delay the ultimate conclusion of this process, it usually leads to engagement, marriage, and a family. Self-consciousness gives way to self-confidence and sexual isolation to sexual intimacy. Quite a change in so few years!

Independence from Home Control

Tween-agers live and die on what their parents think. Everything is considered in light of what Mom and Dad will feel about it. Will they like it or get mad at me for asking? Parents are still the primary security blankets for this age group. In spite of protestations about not caring what they think, parental opinion is more important than anything else at this time in life. Parents provide the tween-ager with their most important role-models and, while this begins to fade at age thirteen or so, Mom and Dad are still too important to be left out of decisions.

As young adults progress through the developmental gauntlet called adolescence, they will, under normal conditions, establish their own basis for relating with parents from outside the parents' circle of influence. Young adults rely on themselves for feelings of security, viewing parents more as friends than sources of security.

If the process of gradual emancipation from parental control is handled properly by the parents, children can become our best friends once they have settled into their adult roles. If we have over-controlled or been abusive with our discipline, we may break the bonding connection and *never* have the kind of adult-to-adult relationship we would like.

Intellectual Maturity

Young teenagers still generally see their parents as more god than human and tend to accept their decisions and comments as gospel. They believe what their parents believe at this age. Even though they desire objective facts when asked to make a decision, these kids will quickly fall back on their parents' advice at the slightest doubt.

Given that young teenaged adults have progressed through most of their formal education by this time, we should expect them to begin making their own decisions. Adults are more willing to consider subjective aspects of things than are young teenagers, and the kind of evidence accepted as valid for settling a dispute varies greatly between these two age groups. In spite of the changes, though, loving and powerful parents will find their influence continuing far beyond these years spent at home. Harsh and punitive parents will find their influence to be primarily negative with equally long-term results.

Occupational Interest

We don't normally think of twelve-and thirteen-year-olds as engaged in the process of career selection. Most kids at this age still want to be in the glamorous occupations such as acting, science, the military, or any of a number of faddish occupations that become popular. It reminds me of a television character who admitted to thinking about a career but still couldn't make up his mind whether to be a brain surgeon or a fry-cook. Our kids are probably beyond that level of indecision, but they still tend to over or underestimate their abilities and aptitudes.

Parents remain a major influence on the occupational preferences of their children. Of course, there are many exceptions, but the idealized memories held over from childhood of what it is to be a man or woman continue to influence our ideas as adults. Books, television, documentaries, and family friends may be strong influences at this time.

Self-Concept

Children and young adolescents tend to identify themselves in terms of family, home, and school. It is in the tween-years that our kids typically begin to move away from this corporate self-concept to one that is more individual and less family-dependent. This age group still has only weak skills in the areas of self-perception and recognizing the motives and goals of others. Self-concept and identity build on what parents have provided in the years preceding this time, and the fruit of their efforts toward raising an independent young person are sometimes surprising. We will say more about identity later, but I want to emphasize the importance of parental ability to distinguish between normal movement toward independence and negative rebellion during the early years of adolescence. Remember, too, that the term "tween-age" is not an exact term. It is more a state of mind reflecting the transition from childhood to adolescence.

Tween-agers develop a truly independent self-concept built on their own preferences and abilities, relating to parents as equals rather than superiors. Their ability to discern their own motives and those of others improves greatly by early adulthood along with a much more accurate and reasonable self-image.

Relationship With God

Tween-agers usually accept the God of their parents without much questioning. Moral decisions about sex, alcohol, drug experimentation, good and bad friends, and even which political party to claim allegiance to in civics class are all based on how parents feel about these things. Often religious awareness is built on fear rather than love and respect for God, since God is still viewed somewhat as a Super-Parent. Salvation is accepted in terms of what parents believe about it, and security is based not in what God says about the subject, but what parents say.

Young adolescents gradually become uncomfortable with this blind acceptance of parental beliefs and, along with with the development of mental abilities that enable them to consider abstract ideas like eternity and an unlimited universe, they become open to the kind of salvation messages they hear at church camps and in Sunday School. Most people accept Christ as children or teenagers. Those who become Christians during childhood often feel compelled to "rededicate" themselves to God during adolescence because of the different level of understanding.

As they move toward full adulthood, a more personal concept of God is developed through a period of questioning parental beliefs. Parents need to develop tolerance for these questions, knowing that they are normal and good, and will ultimately lead to a mature idea of what Christianity is all about.

Usually these young adults view God as love and the fearful aspects of God are lessened. Sometimes this emphasis on the love of God leads young adults into a casual, almost "flip" manner of worship that is particularly upsetting to parents, but this, too, is developmental. It will gradually evolve into worship based on love, dedication, and respect for the God who is powerful enough to create all that is. Salvation becomes a very personal matter during these years, sometimes leading to a second "rededication" to the Lord.

When considering these many areas of development between young adolescence and adulthood, the main challenge is to resist overreacting to the kinds of things outlined above. Much damage is done by loving parents who overreact to these normal steps in the growth of their children, creating a permament chasm between parent and grown child that may never be healed.

It does not have to happen.

If we can trust the Holy Spirit to lead us and our children to make the right final decisions, we will be able to relax and trust God. God does know the beginning from the end (Proverbs 3:5-6; Colossians 2:2-3), and though our kids may have to experience a few hard knocks along the way, God has final authority over these young Christians, not their parents. Influential and powerful as parents are, we are *not* gods and we do not have the final say in what becomes of our children. By trusting God and our godly child-rearing methods, the entire family should be more relaxed and less upset with each other during the years our children grow into adults.

Adolescent Insanity

Parents have a really tough time figuring out their first tween-ager. Kids at this age are going through hormonal and physical changes that defy description, let alone understanding. We are faced with a thirteen-year-old whose body is probably all out of proportion, sprouting pimples from every pore, and feeling incredibly self-conscious.

And we are expected to know what to do with these half-adult, half-child creations?

Although there is very little we can do about the goofiness that seems to go along with early adolescence, we *can* build our understanding so that when the "weirdness" arrives, we will be ready. The next areas we will look at may seem a little silly at times, but they are a real part of the life of tween-agers. Parents can benefit from being prepared and ready.

Hormonal and Biological Adjustments

There is a lot of very strange stuff going on inside the body of a tween-ager. The impact of biological changes is greatest in the first years following the onset of puberty, the early years of adolescence.

In addition to the growth variations mentioned earlier, tween-agers experience all the self-consciousness and embarrassment one might expect from an immature person who looks and feels different. Simple verbal explanations of what is going on will greatly ease your son's or daughter's physical transition from child to adult. Kind assurances from parents that everything *will* turn out all right will eventually take effect.

Reading material on the subject of anatomical and hormonal explanations may be better than father/son or mother/daughter talks. These are different from morality or sex talks. Parents *need* to talk with their young teenagers about sexual decisions and the need for Christ-honoring behavior in all aspects of life, including sex. My experience has shown that when it comes to how they look and feel, though, often impartial reading material presenting factual information is best. After all, these kids know that we love them, and because of that, our judgments about their appearance are bound to be biased in their favor. It really means knowing your child and how he or she would best respond. If you do give them reading material, be available and open if they want to discuss it or get additional information.

Peer Pressure

The self-consciousness we have been discussing leads to a peculiar kind of defense mechanism in younger teenagers. In order to escape the terrible insecurity felt by virtually all in this age group, they will dress, act, and generally try to be like the majority of their friends at school.

This is peer pressure.

It is not a conscious attempt by "someone" to get our kids to conform, but, rather, a force coming from the teenagers themselves. This force tells a teenager he will feel better if he complies in appearance and behavior. Peer pressure causes kids to accept the standards of the age group with whom they associate, but the motivation for conforming is based on the fact that the young person simply feels better as a result. He belongs. This good feeling is very hard to overcome by Christian parents trying to convince their young people to conform to another standard than that which the world offers.

Dealing with peer pressure while retaining God-given power and influence means being tolerant of this need to conform without compromising. Parents need to be re-assured that this self-motivated peer pressure will diminish with age. Parents who do not overreact to hair and clothing in early adolescence can hasten this process. We can do this without being either legalistic or permissive, but it will take a lot of trust in the Holy Spirit to enable us to smile at these temporary forms of strange behaviors while still maintaining family standards acceptable to Christ. Parental lifestyle and modeling are key elements in how a young person will handle this.

Imaginary Audience

There are many reasonable explanations for adolescent behavior. The concept of an imaginary audience is one way to explain the apparent contradiction of a young adolescent being tremendously egotistical and very self-conscious at the same time.

A child's thinking goes something like this: *When I go to school today everybody will notice what I'm wearing (egotism), and because I am so afraid of embarrassing myself by wearing something that will make me look stupid, I'll wear what all the other kids are wearing (self-consciousness) and take no chances.*

Every young teenager is absolutely convinced that he or she is the center of attention all the time and that the other kids are just waiting for an opportunity to point out a flaw and laugh. For instance:

Jenny was already late for school this morning. Her mom couldn't guess what was taking her so long to get out of her room. She knew tenth grade girls were careful about their make-up, but this was getting out of hand.

"Jenny" she called, "get yourself down here right now or you'll miss the school bus."

"I can't go to school today, Mom," she replied. "I have a problem."

Jenny's mom went up to check, expecting to hear the same old story usually reserved for test times about sniffles or a headache.

"What's the matter, are your allergies acting up again?"

"Mom, look at this pimple on my nose. Couldn't you just die! I can't go to school looking like this. All the kids will notice, and I'll be *so* embarrassed."

Jenny's mom looked and could find only a small blemish,

nothing like the major pimple Jenny was complaining about.

"Jenny, no one will notice that small pimple. Don't be silly. Finish getting ready for school."

"Not notice! Mom, this thing is a Vesuvius on my face. I can't go to school like this!"

Vesuvius on my face?

To Jenny, that pimple was as noticeable as a volcano. It wasn't, but *she* was convinced that everybody would notice. Jenny's imaginary audience would not let her go to school until something was done about the pimple on her nose that looked as big as a volcano... to her.

How can parents deal with the imaginary audience?

Tolerance, a sense of humor, and kind, caring feedback from Mom or Dad's viewpoint will usually do the job. Young adolescents are peer oriented, but they still give a lot of weight to parents' opinions and judgments.

Personal Fables

There is not much that is funny about personal fables in adolescence, even young adolescence.

Personal fables are stories, lies we make up about ourselves when we are teenagers in order to avoid confronting the fact that we do not have something other kids have. These begin innocently enough with stories of boyfriends or girlfriends made at summer camp or while spending July with grandparents. These fairy tales may include exciting adventures that never happened, movie stars not really spoken to, or autographs that are really forgeries to impress friends.

But later in adolescence, personal fables take on another, more serious complexion.

Girls will tell themselves that *they* cannot get pregnant with *their* boyfriends, and, after all, it *is* the first time!

A boy will convince himself that automobile accidents can happen to others, but there is really no reason for *him* to wear his seatbelt. Auto accidents may be the leading cause of death in teenage boys, but he knows it won't happen to him!

110

Crazy?

Yes, but that's adolescence.

Every teenager feels immortal. Every teenager feels that what has happened to others will not, *cannot,* happen to him. When a friend is killed in a car wreck or commits suicide, teenagers are devastated. They can't believe it! So for about two weeks everyone wears seatbelts and tries to encourage friends who are acting depressed. Then they go back to seeing themselves as immortal and invincible.

"I won't get pregnant, die in a car accident, catch AIDS, get caught shoplifting, or become addicted to the cocaine I'm fooling around with!"

"Not me!"

Although imaginary audience is almost universal in teenagers, its effects can be controlled by parents who have retained some measure of their power and influence with their kids.

Parents can help teenagers by providing calm, factual information on subjects of concern to their teens. Articles on teenage pregnancy or drug addiction can be clipped out and left on the table for the teenager to read. Dinner table conversation can be steered to subjects in the news like AIDS or the boy in Centerville killed in a head-on collision last night.

Non-accusatory comments and innocent information let the teenager know that Mom and Dad care about them and are willing to help them deal with these issues.

"No, of course we don't think you are going to get pregnant. We know what kind of Christian character you have, but maybe the information could help someone you know."

Kids who do get pregnant or hooked on drugs universally complain that their parents *never* talked to them about it. We can help our kids face difficult questions and moral judgments without believing they are into something. We can provide information without accusing them of doing *anything.*

If we do it in love!

Tween-agers *are* crazy—in a very wonderful kind of way!

111

But parents can enjoy their temporary insanity if we remember that it *is* temporary and if we give them loving, accurate feedback. The volcano on Jenny's nose looked smaller after Mom talked to her. It didn't go away, but she felt better. I know, because Jenny was one of our tween-agers!

Basic Needs of Young Teenagers

The things that tween-agers need most are primarily social concerns. This assumes that their basic physical and spiritual needs are being met by the family. Families where this is not the case will be discussed later. For now, we will assume that food, shelter, and clothing are being taken care of as are needs for basic parental guidance in spiritual and moral areas. As we look at what younger teenagers need, I want to emphasize that these *are needs* rather than desires or wishes.

Adolescents need friends almost as desperately as they need food and water. Teenagers should be encouraged to develop socially, and parents should expect this growth to be reflected in added maturity in dealing with people.

It must also be emphasized that parents cannot choose friends for their teenagers, young or old. What we can do is to choose the group from which our kids will choose their friends. In so doing, we can exercise some power and influence in their lives for their ultimate benefit. We choose the larger group by selecting a school (Christian or public), the neighborhood we live in, where the kids are allowed to gather and socialize, and what the family does as a group.

Adolescents with strong parents who maintain a good Christian testimony without much hypocrisy can fully expect to have less trouble with their teenagers' friends than parents with less power. Teenagers respect power in their parents because it shows caring and concern. As long as the power is appropriate and not smothering, kids will generally accept what their parents are trying to do for them.

Younger teenagers need to expand their social world. They do this by making friends with virtually anyone who will accept them. They will seek out kids from different backgrounds and "collect" as many friends as possible.

Tween-agers make little distinction between friends and acquaintances. Anyone they know and who knows them is a friend. So don't be suprised when your young teenager brings home all manner of young people and introduces them as "friends." They can't help it.

Another need is to find and strengthen an appropriate sex-role. This means simply becoming more "fixed" in their appropriate sex and learning the acceptable bevaviors that go along with it. Hanging out with same sex friends is a rite of passage for young teenagers because it helps establish security in a sex-role for boys and girls.

Recognition and acceptance are strong needs in all adolescents, but most powerful in young teens. Most say "hi" to *everybody* and expect the same in return. This ritual of saying hello to all the other kids works this way psychologically.

"Hi, John how are you doing?" (Say "hi" and recognize my existence, John!)

"Hey, Paul, how's it goin' man?" (Thanks for recognizing that I'm here Paul. I'm happy to do the same for you.)

The social interaction so prevalent in adolescents is important in building self-concept, establishing status among a group, and building security in knowing that these are "my" friends. Shy teenagers *want* to be as gregarious as others, but are afraid to risk looking foolish. The power of friends and fads is as great on the shy teen as on the outgoing one.

Adolescents need to be allowed a certain level of dating experiences. I am not in favor of pushing maturity on kids too early, but young teenagers can be allowed to develop emotional maturity by participating in group activities sponsored by church youth programs. Such things as skating, picnics, games and sports night, and other activities give kids an opportunity to feel like the older teenagers while they get some valuable dating experience under controlled and chaperoned conditions. A good church youth group can save parents a lot of hassle later.

Parents who keep their power and influence with their tween-agers recognize their growth needs for what they are—

normal—and use their parent power to encourage the right kinds of social activities. Our children are supposed to move gradually out of our homes and into their own lives. We should encourage this gradual transition, not fight it.

Common Problems in Families with Young Teenagers

Some families have significantly more trouble raising adolescents than others do. Problems that surface in mid-to-late adolescence begin in early adolescence, and they usually stem from family circumstances and parent behaviors. These few we will look at are the most common and produce the longest lasting turmoil in the family.

Confused Communication

Failure to communicate clearly is a major contributor to parent-teen disputes and misunderstanding. This seems to be most true in the area of rules and limits regarding what young teenagers are allowed to do. Confused communications are at the heart of the pattern known as "we never talk to each other at home." It is not so much an inability to communicate clearly as a lack of understanding as to why it is important.

Families having trouble with teens are often led by parents who do not understand the need for clear communication and may be unable to communicate on an intimate level. Those like this are very hard to convince when changes are in order. What communication there is in troubled families generally falls into the category of commands and corrections rather than normal conversation.

As a general rule, when kids in trouble are asked to list the rules their parents have for them at home, they usually cannot do it. When teenagers not in trouble are asked about the rules at home, there is a clear understanding and ability to state the rules that is distinctive. A pattern of good, clear communications in a family almost guarantees that no major problems will arise.

114

Leadership

God has established the parental system for all families, not just Christian ones. Parents must exercise many abilities in raising their children. Power, discipline, love, safety, nurture, and *leadership* are just a few of the things God expects us to provide for our children.

Fathers seem especially vulnerable to the loss of leadership at home. Remember? To whom more is given, more is expected (Luke 12:48). Fathers and mothers share equal but different leadership responsibilities in the home. When leadership is missing, so is Christian character in the kids.

Our tween-agers are very vulnerable to shortcomings in parents because sex-role identity is becoming fixed. Ineffective parenting can lead to disastrous results later. Leadership and parent power are issues even the liberals are beginning to recognize as crucial to raising good kids. Our model of leadership is Jesus, who led His disciples with love and power. We can do no less for our young teenagers.

Problem-solving

Parents also model the ability to figure out solutions to problems for their children. If Mom and Dad are ineffective in producing solutions for family problems, children and young teenagers can be expected to react with fear, anger, and frustration. If parents cannot solve their financial problems or resolve a moral dilemma, children come to believe that these problems are more or less normal. They become even less effective in solving the same problems when they become adults themselves.

Have your children and teenagers ever heard their parents *pray* about a problem? Have they been allowed to listen in as Mom and Dad resolved a disagreement about something and came out of it smiling? Are there family devotions in the home and are answers to problems discussed in light of Biblical solutions found in God's Word?

When counselors begin working with a family having serious trouble with a younger teenager, we always find one or more of these three family behaviors absent. And it doesn't have to happen! Parents only have to take their responsibilities seriously and determine under God to not let their parent power be siphoned off by the world, by personal weaknesses, or by sin.

Comunication, godly and powerful leadership, and Biblical problem solving are all characteristics found in Christian families who have found the answer to raising teenagers.

Parent Power and Tween-age Popularity

We might as well face it, not all of our kids will be as popular as we or they would like. Since popularity is critical to self-concept in this age group, parents can help by understanding how the process works.

We already know that the most popular teenagers will probably be the best looking, tallest (even for girls), and early maturers. Teenagers who seem to hold the same attitudes as the majority will be elected to class offices, chosen to be cheerleaders and team captains, and generally better liked than others. Popularity in adolescence is often connected very much to appearance and behavior. Frequently, this reflects what parents are like.

When we deal with a teenager who is not popular and who feels miserable because of it, there are some things parents and others can do to help.

First, we can be reminded that popularity is based on personality and appearance, both of which are partially inherited. We can help our teens by encouraging them in the knowledge that *we* made it through adolescence, and so can they. This might sound like a small comfort, but kids at this age are still very dependent on parents for their sense of worth. Telling them that we know what they are like inside may sound corny, but it helps.

We can also help by structuring activities to contradict their negative self-image. Rafting trips and programs like Outward Bound and Summit Expeditions can do wonders for a teen's self-concept. They may not be any more popular, but it will bother them less.

Any adult can help by offering social advice. Social

activities and concerns with popularity are new to the tween-ager. Perhaps there is a certain behavior that could be stopped (dressing in plaids and stripes, a poor hair cut, talking too much, butting in) or started (brushing teeth more often, smiling more, making friends with other, less popular kids) that could help.

In any case, the love and security provided by the right kind of parents will go a very long way to making these early years more pleasant for the tween-ager.

Parents, teachers, and youth workers can help by talking positively about an unpopular teenager in front of the other kids. This plants a seed of doubt in their minds that *maybe* they are being too hard on this person. After all, if the youth director really seems to like him, maybe he isn't so bad after all.

Preparation for Adolescence

The distinction between early and later adolescence often escapes those who do not deal with these two age groups on a regular basis. Parents, teachers, and church youth leaders understand very well that the tween-age years of twelve, thirteen, and maybe fourteen set the pattern for what is to follow. The preparation for dealing with older adolescents, the ones who want to date and drive cars, begins with understanding the needs of younger teenagers and matching the fulfillment of those needs with our responsibilities as Christian parents.

Once tween-agers learn that Mom and Dad love them enough to say yes *and* no, enough to prevent them from doing something harmful to self or others, and enough to stand up to their attempts to usurp parent power, their behavior at fifteen through nineteen or twenty will be much more in line with family principles and more pleasing to God. They are exploring the boundaries of developing adulthood while being flooded with an enormous surge of growth and hormonal changes.

Hang in there! God isn't finished with adolescents of any age. The process of growing up has only just begun.

117

7
POWER PARENTING TEENAGERS

The need for parent power is never stronger than during adolescence. Teenage young people need calm, compassionate guidance from right-living Christian parents more than they need anything else, and they will need this on-going example for several years.

One expert has labeled adolescence a "normative crisis," implying that many crises adolescents go through are more or less normal for that age group. Aristotle called the years of 12-17 "the flu of life," recognizing even in ancient days that this age group is different. Aristotle probably never experienced the many crises today's teenagers face or he might have thought of a more serious affliction than flu to identify with adolescence.

In this part of the twentieth century, adolescence is the most dangerous time of life. Dangerous physically, emotionally, legally, and spiritually. The number one cause of death for American teenagers is automobile accidents. Number two is suicide. If a person is ever going to enter a mental institution, get arrested and convicted for a felony, become pregnant out of wedlock, become addicted to alcohol or other drugs, or become depressed, that person is more likely to experience these things as a teenager than at any other age.

We are concerned about our teenagers because we should be concerned. Adolescence is only carefree fun and games in our memories.

A Brief Look at the History of Adolescence
Adolescence has not always been with us. Not only was it an unknown stage in early Mesopotamia, but as recently as the turn of this century, adolescence was an unknown concept in the minds of the great majority of people. The historical fact is that adolescence was invented during the

early 1900s because of basic changes in American culture, primarily the rise of industrialism and the development of modern machinery.

The concern is that we are acting as if adolescence has always been with us and is a basic and indispensable part of normal human development. We behave as though the *status quo* has always been when, in fact, a dramatic change in the way society viewed youth took place in the period between 1890 and 1920.

What we call adolescence today was created in response to industrialization, more efficient methods of farming, and a general reduction in the number of hands needed in the work place. The least skilled hands were always the first to be replaced by machinery and so it was the youngest workers who had to go.

But where to put them? A cynic once said that the trouble with teenagers is that we don't know what they're good for. Society began to learn that adolescents unoccupied are adolescents at risk, and we began to change compulsory school attendance laws so that the legal age to quit rose from twelve, then to fourteen, and is now sixteen. We brought youths from the farm into the factories that needed vast amounts of unskilled labor. Then they were dropped when advances in machinery made them expendable.

Not only is adolescence a recent invention, but even "childhood" has only been recognized as a special stage in development for the last 150 years or so. I came across a book with the title "The Office of Christian Parents" a while back and discovered very different age-stage designations than those we have today. In this early American seventeenth century book, infancy is designated as the time from birth to seven years of age. (Early primary level classes were called "infant schools.") Childhood was the period from 7-14; youth was from 14 to 28; manhood included the years between 28 and 50; something called "gravity" began at age 50 and lasted until about 70. Old age began at 70, and you can guess when it ended.

Note the total absence of adolescence in the thinking of these early Americans. Youth was the closest to adolescence

119

in meaning but it lasted until age 28! We know that "youth" was a label applied to persons lacking wealth and who were usually apprenticed out by age fourteen, girls often at even younger ages. There are records showing children being sent out from their families as early as seven for training as servants or apprentices.

On the other hand, wealthy children and young people experienced a very different life. When well-to-do young people reached secondary school age, they went off to university to further their tutored education. Some entered a profession like law or medicine, and some went into the family business. There was a time-out for young people in wealthy families that roughly corresponds to what we call adolescence, but this was a rare opportunity reserved for only the privileged few. It in no way resembles the common experience of today's teenagers.

Enough of history for now. The important point is that adolescence has not always been with us and is not experienced even today by most people in other countries, especially non-Western countries. Adolescence is a culturally defined concept, dependent on certain labor-saving technologies that made mass labor obsolete. Society decides when adolescence begins and ends. It will probably change again in our lifetime.

It is important for parents to understand the transient nature of adolescence. It is important for our own peace of mind and for the healthy development of our young people. Adolescence is artificial, a plastic invention visited upon our youth because we did not know what to do with them. Understanding this will enable us to have greater empathy for the frustration, rebellion, anger, and generally erratic behavior we often see in these young people. Our power and influence as parents depends greatly on our ability to see things through the eyes of our kids and to remember what we felt like when we were adolescents.

Roadblocks to Understanding

We parents often have a hard time understanding what our

young people are going through. This awareness we seek keeps bumping into a variety of roadblocks, knowledge vacuums that detour and delay us in our attempts to do and be the best we can for our teenagers. These roadblocks stem from our own upbringing, stereotypes and prejudices, bad learning, and loss of memory about our teenaged years. These obstacles to understanding must be dealt with head-on if we are to realize the power and influence God gave us when we became parents.

One roadblock has to do with our understanding of the history of adolescence, the subject dealt with a few paragraphs ago. The fact is, adolescence is *not* a necessary part of human development.

I remember talking to my grandmother a few years before she died about what it was like to grow up around the turn of the century. She was born in 1895 and married in 1910.

"Oh, David, we didn't have anything like teenagers when I was growing up."

I didn't press the subject then because I thought we were just using different terms. But as I have looked into the subject in the years since, I have realized the truth of what she was telling me. They *didn't* have adolescence when my grandmother was young. In fact, she was married at 15, and gave birth to my father the following year and that was normal for that time in history!

A second obstacle to understanding adolescence for Christians is the fact that adolescence is not recognized as a specific stage of development in the Bible. Apparently, there were *no* adolescents in the Bible times. Oh, there were teenagers of course, defined as such because there were 13, 14, or 17-year-olds, but there were no *adolescents* in those days. David was *not* an adolescent when he went out to fight Goliath. Joseph was *not* an adolescent when he was sold into slavery by his jealous brothers. They were young *men.* They were *not* old children.

When we look to the Bible for answers to life, as we should, we must understand that there was no special time between childhood and adulthood. Those we would call adolescents today were called "youths," "young men," and "maids." When we apply Biblical principles to dealing with adolescents today, we must use those passages that speak of dealing with *people* generally. The Bible is not short on answers about dealing with teenagers, but sometimes we are short on understanding the historical context of the Bible.

We also experience problems understanding the difference between an adolescent's role and his status. A role is what we expect from a teenager. Status refers to levels of independence and responsibility.

We allow 16-year-olds to drive $12,000 automobiles capable of traveling at speeds over 100 miles an hour, but we won't let them choose what television programs to watch. They can make choices about what courses to take in school and what college to attend, but they have to check with us before they go to a friend's house.

Something's strange about this, and our kids know it.

In addition to the confusion over role and status, there is the problem with feeling inferior. Part of the problem is that teenagers *are* subordinate to adults, and they know it. Their normal cravings for independence are often stifled because of that overwhelming self-consciousness we discussed in the last chapter, a shyness that stems from feeling inferior to adults. Much of their anger and frustration surfaces following yet another blow to their already weak self-concepts. Building teenagers up by emphasizing their strong points is one of the best ways parents can help their children *and* maintain their God-given power and influence.

Then, there is the problem of growing up in a rapidly changing world, one that seems to create new problems almost daily. These closing years of the twentieth century do present more problems and more complicated situations to be dealt with than any experienced by our children's parents. It *was* easier to be an adolescent when I was growing up than it is now for my youngsters. Simply recognizing that is a major step in becoming really understanding of our teenagers.

Understanding the Parent's Perspective

It's also imperative to consider parents when trying to

understand adolescence. Parents are normally defensive regarding their children and reluctant to admit problems when they surface. This tendency is natural and is only a serious problem when it is not recognized for what it is. I don't want outsiders meddling in my family and neither do you, but *sometimes* we have to rethink this attitude when it comes to getting help with a serious problem involving our kids.

Parents are sometimes confused about what it is that teenagers want. The comment I hear from parents is, "What do they want from us anyway?" From their teenager I get, "I wish I could figure out what Mom and Dad expect from me." When parental amnesia sets in, parents of teenagers forget what *they* wanted when they were young. Confusion results. We will look at specific goals of teenagers a little later in this chapter.

Another reason for the importance of understanding yourself as a parent is that Mom and Dad are changing, too, and sometimes these changes are not pleasant. A mother experiencing menopause or a father beginning to recognize his former athletic build is rapidly sinking into the sunset come face to face with teenagers who look their best, are at their peak in energy and strength, but who complain all the time.

"What do you have to complain about?" asks balding and winded dad of his athletic 16-year-old. . . .the 16-year-old who can't understand why Dad doesn't want to play tag football anymore.

And, then, there are all the attacks on the nuclear family unit to face. Everybody is getting a divorce, or so it seems, and Christian parents wonder if *they* are vulnerable in some unknown way. Teenagers want more money *and* more independence, all at the same time. Parents get conflicting messages from "experts" and from preachers, from their parents and their friends. Parents need a time out occasionally to regroup and get their heads together before rejoining the turmoil of raising adolescents. Attacks on the family unit can be repelled, but it takes a united front to accomplish it.

How Teens Change

The challenge for parents and their teenagers is to adjust to and benefit from the changes of adolescence. Lack of preparation leads to problems for parent and teen alike. These problems left uncorrected will likely grow in seriousness. We want to see these changes as inevitable and healthy, leading the way for our young people to become fully functioning Christian adults.

Physiologically

When puberty strikes, things begin to change. The magnitude of the physical and sexual changes following puberty are rivaled only by infancy. But more important than the physiological changes themselves is the young person's ability to adjust to the growth and maturation. Body image, athletic abilites, self-concept, sexual awareness, all these impact the developing self of the adolescent and lead eventually to an acceptance of that self as a complete physical adult.

Intellectually

Jean Piaget, the world famous Swiss child psychologist, called adult thought "formal operations thinking," assumed to be the highest level of thought for human beings. The primary characteristic of this level of adult thinking is the ability to deal with abstractions. Creativity often accompanies movement into this stage but not always. Death awareness, the sense of God in each of us, these also represent movement to adult levels of thought and understanding.

Attitudes

Teenagers constantly change their attitudes about a whole range of things. How parents are perceived, how authority figures are to be dealt with, what to do about personal responsibility and moral decisions, what is good and bad and what is in between. Their attitudes are in a continual process of revision and adjustment to new circumstances and new learning.

Emotional Adjustments

What is a teenager to do with all these new, strange feelings and urges? The teenager must deal with anger, passion, rejection, frustration, loneliness, and failure on a scale not experienced in childhood, and it's difficult. Parents need to pray for an extra measure of patience and tolerance when their teens begin to experience new emotions.

Personal Adjustments

The challenge is to begin to deal with friends and family in a way that neither important group is alienated, angered, or ignored. Family dynamics is a particular problem for adolescents. Living in an almost adult body with an almost adult brain but still being told to kiss your grandmother good-bye and to clean up your room is stressful. The teenager must learn to do what the family is doing, adjust to himself, and do it in a way that will keep Mom and Dad happy.

Vocationally

It is during these turbulent years that occupational realism reaches up and grabs the teenager's attention. Working in the pizza place or the gas station provides valuable work experience and reveals likes and dislikes previously unknown even to the teenager himself. Academic courses must be chosen with the end goal of a job in the back of his mind and unrealistic, glamorous, exciting occupations go out the window for most teens. The teenager begins to think that maybe Dad's job doesn't sound so bad after all!

Academically

The importance of education slowly dawns on all but the most confused adolescents. Those who wanted to major in cheerleading or fundamentals of surfboard construction begin to realize the limited income producing potential of these fun-sounding occupations. Generally, advice is sought seriously from counselors and parents on what courses to take in order to qualify for this college program or that job requirement. A teen's perception of these things usually changes dramatically between the freshman and senior years in high school.

Moral Issues

Christian parents often have a hard time accepting this

area of change because it can look so negative from a parent's perspective. What is usually going on, though, is normal striving for adult moral understanding in exactly the same manner as they struggle for adult intellectual understanding. Questioning does not necessarily mean rebellion, an important topic we will look at in some detail a little later in this chapter.

How Parents React

Many of the changes we noted present problems for parents. Parents expect to experience a smooth transition from childhood to adulthood when they believe they have done a pretty good job with the kids. So when a teenager expresses some otherwise normal teenage behavior, like challenging previously accepted rules or trying to see how far Mom and Dad's tolerance will stretch before breaking, parents react to what they see as a failure in parenting.

Christian parents are not immune to this sense of failure, and we tend to react in one of three ways. (1) We capitulate, give in, surrender, and hope for the best. (2) We get legalistic and rigid, assuming that when a rule doesn't work or a punishment doesn't correct, it is because it is not strong enough or strict enough, the old "lock 'em in the fruit cellar" method of discipline. (3) We compromise and negotiate, recognizing these power-plays by our teens as more or less normal attempts to establish clear but changing boundaries.

Let's examine how each type of parental reaction fits into the power parenting idea.

Parents who capitulate and give in make a very strong statement about their power. There is a great need for "line drawing" in every Christian family. All children *should* be raised by Christian parents who really believe, "as for me and my house, *we* will serve the Lord" (Joshua 24:15). Parents who give in to the whining and pestering of adolescent youngsters (or toddlers!) sow the seeds of future attacks on their authority. I have never seen it fail!

Children and teenagers are *never* satisfied with a "temporary" surrender by their parents and will *always* come back for more. Why shouldn't they? Parents who surrender tell their children that there is a power vacuum in this family and if parents are not going to fill it, the teenagers and children will. You can count on it!

On the other hand, parents who go to the other extreme of legalistic rigidity are sending the same message in a different language. Parents who depend on legalism for their authority tell their children by their rigid intolerance that they do not trust themselves or their teenager enough to sit down and discuss the matter unless, of course, the kids promise to do whatever Mom and Dad say before hand.

Legalistic parents rely on rules and regulations to do what they do not trust themselves to do—guide and direct the behavior of their children and teenagers. If I am devoid of ideas or afraid to try something new as a means of raising my youngsters, and if I am a Christian, I *will* become legalistic in my parenting. Parents who don't trust their own God-given judgment usually rely on legalism as a rationale for their decisions.

Then there are those Christian parents who have the ability to compromise and negotiate with their teenagers. Keeping in mind the absolute necessity for line-drawing, experience shows that the ability to sit down with unhappy teens and *negotiate* a settlement is a rare skill found only in the most sensitive Christian families.

When I talk about this subject in my child or adolescent psychology classes, almost always one or two college students will stay after to talk with me. It usually goes something like this:

"Why do you suppose my parents were so unwilling to listen to me? I wasn't radical, but just the suggestion of discussing an important issue like dating or movies seemed to drive my parents up the wall. They wouldn't even let me bring the subject up. Why were they afraid to talk things over with me?"

I wish I had an answer that would satisfy them. There is no way for an outsider to explain why parents are so unwilling to talk and negotiate with their teeangers. I think we sometimes see our willingness to talk things over as a sign of weakness when, in fact, it is a sign of strength. We will say more about this later when we discuss discipline, but the ways we parents find to lose our power are really amazing.

The Adolescent Identity Crisis

What is identity anyway?

And why does finding an identity have to be related to a crisis?

The concept of an identity crisis was developed by Erik Erikson. He identified adolescence as the state of "Identity *versus* Role Confusion." In *Childhood and Society,* Erikson hypothesized that each adolescent in a culture like ours faces a choice, a "crisis," regarding what kind of identity to establish for himself. The struggle to establish an independent identity separate from, but not necessarily in opposition to, one's family becomes a major focus of what is called "growing up in America."

We looked at the foundations for self-concept and identity in the previous chapter. During the primary years of adolescence, identity is built on early foundation and is "finished" through a teenager's attempts at resolving several crises. For good or ill, a decision must be reached by the adolescent regarding seven conflict areas. Each offers a positive and a negative option.

Role Experimentation or Role Fixation

We expect teenagers to experiment with many kinds of roles, ranging from the super-good student to the hopeless greaser and everything in between. A teenager in America tries on different roles and personalities like we try on clothing and for about as long. The freedom to try new roles is important even for Christian kids because they have the same psychological need to experiment. Christian parents are especially burdened with the responsibility to allow *some* experimentation while keeping it within safe limits. Safe limits, of course, mean that some things *cannot* be experimented with such as drugs or sex. Limits and boundaries vary between families, and there is a difference in degree or level. However, things the Word of God forbids are never options for experiences "just to see what it's like." To be sure, though, our kids need to think through their convictions for themselves. Once they do, they "own" them. Decisions are then based on God's Word, not simply on what Mom, Dad, or the church says.

If a young person experiences a smothering of this legitimate, not harmful, need to experiment, he or she is likely to "fixate," get stuck, on a level of maturity short of what parents would like. This is the common explanation for a young person from a good Christian family, but one that is legalistic and authoritarian. He may try every sin known to man as soon as he or she is out from under parental domination. Role experimentation at sixteen is much preferred to role experimentation at twenty-six.

Time Perspective or Time Confusion

Adolescents are expected to acquire an appreciation for the importance of history, an understanding of the flow of time even if it is limited to their own lives to this point. This means not only recognizing one's early finiteness, but also becoming aware of the continuum of life. This understanding usually appears around fifteen or so and expresses itself in gradual expansion of awareness and sensitivity about personal mortality.

Ideological Commitment or Confusion of Values

Going back to the experimentation issue, we want to recognize the need in adolescents to make up their own minds about values. This need necessarily involves some questioning and challenging of family beliefs and philosophy that is really very healthy. Virtually every Christian teenager, at one time or another, asks for permission to try another church or to associate with kids from backgrounds very different from his own.

Parents must not let themselves get upset with this. Allowing some questioning and experimentation tells young people that we have confidence in what we believe and are not afraid to have our values held up for comparison. When we forbid discussion of certain subjects related to family values

129

and prohibit contact with "different" people, the message received by our teenagers is that of a lack of confidence.

Parental values *will* be dominant in the lives of their children, and they will be more obvious and solid if we demonstrate that we know what we believe, why we believe it, and that we are not afraid to discuss the subject or allow contact with other ideas. Values confusion generally shows itself in adulthood and usually results from over-controlling parents who were unwilling to allow exploration of new ideas when the time was right.

Self-Certainty or Self-Consciousness

Self is an over-blown concept in present day Christianity. The number of books on the subject reveals how little we know about the role of self from God's perspective and our own self-centeredness. But that is not the subject here. We are talking about developing (1) the belief that we have a reasonable chance of succeeding in life, and (2) a contentment with our place in life.

Teenagers are expected to develop self-confidence during this time in life, a certainty about what they are capable of doing as well as what is outside the realm of possibility. To balance self between egotism and worm-of-the-earth humility is the challenge for adolescents. Given the number of adults still seemingly struggling with this issue, they can use all the help they can get from parents.

Occupational Optimism or Work Paralysis

Adolescents should work during their high school years. It may only be a few hours a week, and it must be balanced against the needs of school, sports, family, and church, but work is good for most teenagers. Having the opportunity to try out different jobs expands skill levels and interests, teaches social skills and occupational knowledge, and builds self-confidence.

When jobs are not available or not allowed, teenagers are retarded in all the areas just mentioned and tend to have a more chaotic adult work experience as a result. The self-discipline of the work place cannot be duplicated at home. Learning about jobs, self, and people are also missed. Part-time work is good for most teens.

Authority Acceptance or Authority Confusion

Whoever came up with the idea that followership comes before leadership knew what he was talking about. In adolescence, authority issues come to the surface with a bang, often devastating parents in the process. Teens have problems accepting authority from *anyone,* teachers, parents, even the police at times.

But resolving the need to follow before leading also includes accepting personal responsibility. Taking orders on the job is prefaced by the ability to see oneself as having responsibility for that job. If there are problems with teenagers accepting authority in school, it is probably because they do not see that they have any role in the decision-making process.

If a young person never comes to grips with followership, leadership later on is out of the question. Parents have a vital role to play here in not letting adolescents off the hook when it comes time to take responsibility and live up to an agreement. More important still is the modeling parents do for their teens. If we behave in such a way as to inspire imitation from our youngsters, the battle is won!

Sexual Polarization or Sexual Confusion

Adolescence is the time of life when sexuality becomes important. Not sexual activity, but sexual identity.

Sexual polarization means becoming firmly established on one end or the other of the sexual continuum. Developing a sense of being male or female without what some have called "bisexual confusion" is the real sexual challenge of the teenage years. Knowing what is expected of a male or a female and feeling competent to live up to those expectations results in sexual polarization, the norm for most people even today.

Adolescent identity should be desired by Christian parents,

not feared. Once an individual identity is established, the young person should be able to face a sinful world confident in who he or she is, who God is, and the unlimited nature of their power source.

Sexual confusion results when the young person finds himself or herself somewhere more toward the middle of that line stretching between male and female. In this case, the middle is total androgeny or no sexual distinctiveness at all, something that doesn't really exist. It is this lack of polarization and the resulting sexual confusion that leads toward homosexuality for males and females.

Sexual confusion results from many factors including home situation, the presence or absence of either parent while growing up, early experiences involving sex, and a multitude of others. It is clear that sexual confusion has no place in the life of a Christian and is dealt with specifically in many portions of Scripture (James 1:13-15; I Corinthians 6:9-10; Romans 1:24-32; Leviticus 20:13). Homosexuality and other forms of sexual confusion have life-changing impacts for people in general and even greater potential for long-term damage for Christians.

Adolescent Conformity

Many think that any group of people sharing a set of beliefs or behaviors *must* be conformists, or they wouldn't all be doing the same thing. Christian adolescents face a special burden because their normal reactions to peer pressure make them look like conformists without even trying.

What should Christian parents know about conformity to help them deal with their teenagers?

First, people are not conformists just because they think or act alike. There are many behaviors engaged in by a majority of the population simply because they are traditional or convenient. The fact that we all believe in a round earth does not make us conformists. The fact that men in our culture wear trousers instead of skirts does not make most men conformists. Shared behaviors alone is not sufficient for the label of conformity.

But teenagers are different in this regard. Adolescents *are* conformists by nature, but it is a developmental occurrence that will level off in strength and eventually diminish as they attain adult status. Parents can help by understanding that the pressure to conform is powerful on American teens. It needs to be recognized, smiled at, dealt with, and added to our knowledge base when we deal with other teens later. Parents who have modeled positive Christian living will see the same amount of peer pressure exerted on their kids as on others, but they will also see a more measured and less frantic response by their adolescents. Good parenting covers a multitude of peer pressures.

Why Parents and Teens Fight

Arguments and disagreements are common occurrences in most families which include adolescents. Fighting and arguing usually stem from normal attempts by teenagers to establish some independence so they can feel more grown up. These family power-plays are often threatening to parents because we don't understand that the motivation for them is normal and good, even though the arguing is unpleasant.

Conflicts between parents and adolescent is as normal as a teenager's messy room, and usually just about as dangerous.

So why do we fight?

We fight because our teenager is becoming an adult, and we have a hard time accepting that fact. We argue over school, family relationships, social activities, responsibility, and morality. We argue because we love our kids and want the best for them. Often we do not understand that their normal struggle for independence and growth is impossible to set aside just to please parents.

School

In junior and senior high school, the primary parental issue is usually grades. Younger teens often fail to appreciate the importance of good grades and are easily tempted to place social events, friends, and fun before study. Some teens tend to have a variety of aches and pains leading to the, "gee Ma, I

133

don't feel so good this morning" routine. Getting teenagers to go to school on time, turn in their assignments, and show respect for teachers seems like something parents take for granted, but not so their adolescents.

School often becomes an unpleasant place for kids. This happens because they may feel rejected and unpopular, or just feel like a loser academically. We can help by remembering what it was like when we were in school and how those little things used to bother us so much. This is a very turbulent period in their lives socially, mentally, and emotionally.

Family Relationships

Family dynamics undergo dramatic changes when children become adolescents. All of a sudden, the family that was once made up of Mom, Dad, and four little kids has become Mom, Dad, and perhaps two pre-teens and two teenagers!

Everything has changed!

The children are becoming young adults. They look more like adults, eat like *ten* adults, want to borrow the car, and actually seem to have some opinions of their own. Then, painfully, sometimes we realize that our kids are becoming smarter than we are, learning things in school that weren't even taught in the "olden days," as teenagers like to label the youth of their parents.

Parents bear the primary burden of adjusting to their growing teens and of being able to accept their new semi-adult status. Special problems are created when the oldest child becomes an adolescent leaving the other kids still mired in childhood or the nether world of the "tween-ager." The first teen in the family wants privileges and freedoms that parents are inexperienced in giving. It is important for parents to look at their child's age, maturity, lifestyle and evaluate each new request on its own merits. Trying to force growing young people to remain within the restrictions of childhood will breed resentment, anger, and sometimes rebellion. If we can only conquer the parental paralysis that afflicts us all at times, we can make the necessary adjustments and enjoy the growth and development of our children.

134

Social Activities

The friends our teenagers choose will concern us as much or more than anything else. Because we were teenagers once ourselves, we become suspicious and tend to worry about the kids with whom our teenagers associate. We know that peers affect even Christian teenagers, and we seek ways to retain our influence in their social world.

One thing at least is certain. Our teenagers will choose friends and activities consistent with what they have been raised to believe is acceptable. Yes, they might sneak off once in a while and do something they know is wrong, but in the long run, parental modeling by consistent Christian parents will pay important dividends.

We need to offer advice and exert pressure when needed, and we must not give our kids the impression that we *expect* them to do wrong. Remember, parents cannot choose friends for their teenagers, but we *can* choose the group from which *they* will choose their friends. A church with a good, active youth ministry is vital. God does not expect us to surrender our power and influence when our kids become adolescents.

Responsibilities

Here we go again, talking about responsibility. The reasons behind an adolescent's reluctance to clean rooms, do chores on time, and fulfill obligations at home are twofold.

First, adolescents often *are* lazy. They expend massive amounts of energy in their activities, as their food intake verifies. They have a hard time understanding why it is necessary to do what is expected *now* when they don't feel like it and the unmade bed isn't going anywhere. I'm afraid most of us are simply going to have to ask God for patience as we continue to strive for obedience, all the while recognizing that laziness is a passing stage within adolescence.

The second has to do with those needs for independence mentioned earlier. There is something in the heart of a normal adolescent, usually beginning around fifteen, that resents being told what to do. It doesn't matter who does the telling, teenagers begin to resist reminders of responsibility.

What's a parent to do?

We can begin by deciding on essentials. Linda and I disagree greatly on the relative value of a tidy room. My feeling is that if the teen wants to live in a room that looks like a hampster cage, let him. At some point *he* will decide that the room smells like old sweat socks and needs cleaning. Clothes on the floor cease to be a problem when Mom washes *only* those items found in the laundry hamper. When friends stop by and see the incredible mess in his room, *he* will be embarrassed and will do something about it.

When orders are given in a Christian home, they must be obeyed. But parents can reduce tension in the home by deciding on what rules are really important and which can be set aside in order to achieve a smoother home operation. Major on the major issues and put minor issues aside during adolescence.

Morality

For purposes of our discussion, we will use the definition in Webster's *New Collegiate Dictionary:* "of or relating to principles of right and wrong in behavior."

There are no minor issues of morality when the moral expectations are Biblically based. For example, a common moral battleground between parents and teenagers involves attending church and Sunday School. I usher where most of our junior and senior high schoolers sit during church services. I have learned many things from this experience, not the least of which is that Christian teenagers do not go to church to meet God; they go to meet their friends.

If your young person is resisting church, is it because there is not an active youth group? Our kids wanted to go to midweek prayer service even when Linda or I had another commitment because it was *fun* for them. They actually enjoyed Wednesday evening prayer service! We can help our kids by choosing a church where they feel comfortable, wanted, and have a good time while learning about God.

Other moral issues relate primarily to parental modeling. No other area of child-rearing so clearly reflects the power of

God in our lives than morality. I have been impressed over the years with the number of young people raised in good Christian homes who strayed during adolescence, perhaps even getting deeply involved in some sin or other, but who *came back* like the prodigal son.

Adolescent Sex-Role Development

Information about the body a person is born into comes very early in life. Most experts agree that the majority of sexual development occurs prior to entering school and well before adolescence. If this is true, why should we be talking about adolescent sex-role development?

Adolescence is the time of life when sex-role learning becomes consolidated and focused, resulting in an interest in the opposite sex, dating, engagement, marriage, and children. The teen years begin the process that will culminate in a normal sexual life for the rest of one's life. Adolescence is the time when we put into practice all we have learned about sex from a variety of sources and match that learning with the modeling we have experienced with our parents.

General Considerations

It is easy to forget what we thought about sex when we were teenagers. We remember how interested we became and when and how we dealt with it, but we tend to forget the uncertainties and lack of self-confidence when we were expected to deal with the opposite sex. Let's look at a couple of points in that regard.

There is no doubt that the body is ready for sex before the mind, emotions, and personality. The Bible says that it is better to marry than to burn (I Corinthians 7:9), but our society insists on neither. Marriage is out of the question in most families until the kids are in their early twenties. *And,* because we are Christians, we are prohibitive about premarital sex. I am not seeking license to do what God prohibits. Rather, what is needed is simple understanding from parents when their young people want to get married.

We must recognize that God does not owe any of us an

137

explanation. He has ordained the system in which we live today and because He is sovereign, we can be confident that He will provide for those young people who are serious about maintaining their testimony while waiting for marriage. God never asks more of us than we can handle (I Corinthians 10:13; II Corinthians 12:9-10).

Sources of Sex-Role Information

The American culture provides two primary sources of sexual information. Parents are a primary source even today because of the power of early experiences on later attitudes and behavior. It is through our parents that we are able to internalize personality characteristics, attitudes, and values. We learn by watching our parents deal with each other. If Dad is a macho gorilla, you can bet Junior will have strong tendencies to be the same. If Mom is the image of a perfect Christian wife and mother, no lesson could be better for her daughters. We absorb the words and actions of our parents about what is good, bad, or neutral regarding sex and sexual interactions. It is these impressions which last.

A second source is the culture itself. Messages from the variety of media bombard our kids *and us* with their messages of, "if it feels good do it." It is a message whose impact is confirmed by the premarital pregnancy rate, the proliferation of pornography, and the breakdown in the family.

Society and its tentacles become stronger every year, and we should not be suprised to see the gradual decay of moral standards we once thought could never change. Movies, television, and the print media are growing stronger every day in their ability to influence our kids. The testimony of godly Christian parents *(plural)* is the number one weapon God intended for our use in winning this battle.

Research on Sexual Development

Beyond generalities, researchers studying the process of learning and sex-role have come up with some very definite and important findings. Christian parents should pay close attention to what we know *for sure* about the process.

First, we know that males tend to be influenced most

strongly by the culture. Females are far more likely to make an identification with their mother whereas boys are more likely to be influenced by movies and television. When girls are interviewed and tested, it is discovered that they want to be like Mom. Boys, on the other hand, are less likely to want to be like their dads and more likely to want to be like John Wayne, or a variety of athletic heroes.

We also know that both boys and girls identify more closely with mother than father. This situation is an advantage for daughters but a disadvantage for sons if dad is not around. It is also a normal and expected occurrence since the responsibility of caring for babies is usually reserved for Mom.

Researchers also found that boys have more difficulty achieving same sex identification. The evidence for this is found in homosexuality statistics. These show at least nine times as many males as female homosexuals and that males are much more likely to get arrested for sexual crime and be more in need of therapy for some degree of sexual confusion.

Males are more anxious about their sex-role than females. This is revealed in the attempts, especially among adolescents and young adult males, to make a statement about their sexual power in the way they dress, walk, talk, and the cars they buy. In this same regard, males show more hostility toward females than vice versa. Locker room talk shows wide variations between males and females.

We learn many things from scientists and researchers about sexual development, but one finding remains dominant. What we are as parents has more influence on how our children deal with their own sexuality and that of others than anything else. Straight parents are most likely to produce straight kids.

Dating: Maintaining Parental Influence

Dating is good for teenagers. It should be controlled and guided, but dating at an age when parents believe the young person is ready to handle some responsibility is a normal and necessary part of growing up. Dating should be controlled but not discouraged! We want to examine here, briefly, the idea of allowing kids to date, but not forcing them to do so. They may not want to date yet, or may not get asked. Understanding this and the pressure is an important aspect of the parental role.

There is no set age at which we should allow our teens to begin dating. Maturity is too individual to allow this kind of generality. We do know that about 12% of high schoolers do not date at all; 36% date only occasionally; 22% date once a week or less; 21% date two or three times a week, and only 9% date more than three times a week.

Dating is important because it fosters maturity, builds social skills, and teaches decision-making. For Christian young people, a church youth group can be a lifesaver for those who want to date but whose parents insist on a controlled situation. Church group dating reduces pressure on younger teens to go to rock concerts and other activities unacceptable to many Christian parents. Dating in groups provides status with a minimum of risk. It also provides older Christian young people opportunities to meet others with similar beliefs and often includes Bible studies on biblically oriented mate selection. Many things of this nature can be dealt with on an outing or in Sunday School class that would not be appropriate from the pulpit. As we have said, dating and group activities meet important needs in the life of an adolescent or young adult, needs which ought not to be overlooked.

Among the important needs met by the dating experience is simple recreation—just having fun with other young people. More importantly in the long run is the building of personal self-concept based on knowing that he or she is datable, fun to be with, and acceptable to others on a social level.

The needs for independence, responsibility, and trust are met by the opportunity to be with people not under a parent's supervision, and feeling more grown up by being away from the family for a time. Social skills are usually acquired and developed as a result of dating as well as learning more about

140

dealing with different people and situations that cannot come from books.

Courtship, engagement, and marriage generally conclude the process of dating. We know from research and experience that the most solid marriages, Christian or otherwise, are those whose partners had wide dating experiences during adolescence. Withholding dating privileges may make parents feel more secure, but the negative payoff often arrives years later in unhappy marriages or premarital affairs.

Conclusion

We have looked at an abundance of material in this chapter, probably more than anyone could absorb in one reading. But take comfort from this: The testimony and character you display before your children every day of their young lives is more influential, powerful, and important than anything the world can throw at them. Follow the leading of the Holy Spirit as you attempt to answer those questions not clearly defined in the Bible, secure in the knowledge that if your life is in order, you will convey the right message to your kids.

Adolescence does seem to be the "flu of life" in many cases. Maybe in most cases. But you can help your teens get through this stage of life, the most dangerous they will ever know, with a minimum of hassle and damage. Who knows? If you're not careful, you might even enjoy raising teenagers!

8
POWER-FULL
SINGLE PARENTING

The truth of the statement, "It takes two to make a marriage but only one to make a divorce" has hit me over and over as I have had the opportunity to work with Christian parents struggling to overcome the effects of divorce. It seems the divorce rate is on the increase even in the Christian community although solid figures on so sensitive a subject are difficult to obtain.

If you have not gone through a divorce, use the information in this chapter to help those in your church or family who have. You will have no trouble finding people who have experienced a divorce.

My primary concern has been the children of divorce, and it is on that subject this chapter focuses. Most of the counseling I do with children and teenagers follows some kind of marital disruption. Divorce, long-term separation, and serious marital fighting take a heavy toll on the mental and spiritual well-being of children and teenagers. When parents dissolve a marriage, much of a child's sense of security is dissolved as well. When security is threatened, children and teens strike back at the source of their trouble, their parents, with remarkable power and intensity.

Even when the home situation is not what it should be, even when the family is in terrible shape, children and teens would rather keep the troubled family together than lose one of their parents. They do not understand the issues from an adult perspective, generally. All they know is that Mom and Dad don't like each other anymore, so *we* have to suffer because one of them is leaving.

However, raising kids alone is *not* a hopeless task *if* we know about the special problems they are likely to experience, and *if* we know what to do when these problems surface.

This chapter supplies the information and awareness parents need to raise children following divorce. If you are a single parent reading this, I want you to know that I am aware of what you are going through. But I also know that divorce trauma is a time-limited problem in most cases, and there are things we can share that will help you through the process. If you have experienced a divorce, no matter who was primarily at fault, you are probably feeling guilty, isolated, and unable to raise your children properly.

Two to make a marriage, only one to make a divorce! But there are answers to your problems. God promises never to leave us nor forsake us. He will supply the information and sensitivity we need to get through a crisis and grow from it if we will ask.

Power in single-parenting is a realistic goal. The realization of that power is based, in part, on having the necessary information on how to do the job and, in part, on asking God to give you the strength to implement what you learn. You may be a single parent, but you are not isolated from God's provision and protection. It is 100% available to you.

Impact of Divorce

Divorce impacts members of the family in different ways. We are focusing on children in this chapter, but a few words about what happens to divorced parents might be helpful.

Divorced people are at risk for virtually everything negative. This fact is especially true of divorced fathers who have lost or surrendered custody of their children. Automobile accidents, admissions to mental hospitals, addiction to drugs and alcohol, developing cancer and other medical problems, even suicide are much higher in divorced people. Divorce is a stressful event under the best of circumstances.

Christian parents are less likely to get involved in drugs and alcohol following a divorce, but there is still the guilt issue to handle. Not only have we participated in creating great problems for our children, but we may also have violated

Biblical principles as well. Even parents who are victims of the sin of husband or wife feel guilty about the separation or divorce. We feel as if there *must* have been another way to solve the problem. We say, "Maybe I should have given in to what he wanted," or, "maybe I should have been more understanding of her needs," and we forget that there is no permission to sin. You may not have been the best husband or wife, but you are *not* responsible for the sin of another human being, spouse or not.

A divorced Christian parent can do one thing for his or her children that will help them more than anything else. Do not punish yourself and accept guilt for what your spouse did. If you were at fault, confess it to God and ask His forgiveness. Then get on with the original job He gave you of raising *His* children.

Power and self-induced guilt are absolutely incompatible. You cannot have them both at the same time, and your children need your power and influence now more than ever.

Divorce Impact on Children

One fact that will remain constant as we look at different problems and different age groups is that 92% of divorced children live with Mom. Because of that statistic, I am speaking as though the mother has the children. When Dad has the children, some things change, but because this is still an infrequent occurrence, the differences have not been well studied.

Birth to Two Years

Infants will not understand that a member of their family is absent. Children at this age are generally very adaptable and will only react if they sense emotional stress in Mom. Therefore, divorcing parents of an infant should pay special attention to providing smooth routines and keeping the baby insulated from whatever emotional upset is being experienced.

Babies care a lot if Mom leaves, but when Dad leaves, they hardly notice. One study found that the average father spends less than *one minute per day* in face to face interaction with

144

infants younger than three months. Dad becomes very important later, but if Mom gets custody, we usually don't see any kind of separation anxiety in infants.

Often day-care becomes necessary following a divorce. Infants handle this new experience better than any other age group, and they do particularly well if they have the same caregiver every day. We looked at issues of day-care in an earlier chapter, so I will just re-emphasize that day-care can be a very good experience if the facility is carefully chosen.

Boys in the 18-to-30 month age group sometimes have night terrors for a few months after Dad leaves. This can be handled in several ways. However, the child should not be allowed to sleep in Mom's bedroom or in Mom's bed. This is important because the tendency is to settle for a short-term solution to a bad dream without considering more important long-term problems that can be created. Another partial solution is to increase contact with the father. This reassures the child that Dad is still there and is still his father. This is not an expected occurrence but, when it does happen, the impact of divorce dissipates rapidly in most cases.

Two to Three Years

Typical post-divorce reactions of toddlers include various forms of regression to a younger form of behavior. Loss of toilet training is common, as is a return to dependence on security symbols such as a favorite blanket or thumb sucking. Toddlers are likely to become irritable, especially if Mom is under pressure or is experiencing anxiety. Older toddlers often become aggressive to younger brothers and sisters. Tantrum behavior becomes more frequent as well.

Most parents underestimate the ability of their younger children to understand and use information about what is going on and why. In fact, the most severe post-divorce reactions we see in young children occur in those famliies where no explanation is given. Young children are resilient. They have an amazing capacity to bounce back from all kinds of tragedies, but when we do not give them enough information so as to allow understanding, the crisis continues

145

for them. It is only when they have some degree of understanding of what is happening and what it means for them that they can make the needed adjustments.

Three to Five Years

You will recall that it is during these years children make their most important attachments to a male or female role. Boys with father loss prior to age six have more trouble establishing a masculine identity than boys with father loss after age six. Girls are less likely to experience difficulties in this area because most will still be living with their mother.

Another major problem at this age is that many parents tend to use their children for their own needs following the divorce. The ideal pattern of parent-child emotional contact is parent *to* child, not the reverse. When Mom (or Dad) begins to depend on preschoolers for the majority of the love and affection he or she gets, problems are just around the corner. Children of both sexes are likely to be more disobedient when only one parent is in the home, but boys are greater problems primarily because of the lack of sex-role models.

Moving into the parental bed is a common desire for preschool aged children, but when this is allowed, serious obstacles to later emotional maturity develop. Boys and girls who are allowed to sleep with Mom in the absence of Dad are known to be less mature both socially and emotionally when entering school. Boys suffer a greater deficit in maturity than girls.

Of major importance is telling the child over and over again that he or she is not responsible for the divorce. Many young children, and older ones, too, will assume that if they had been a better boy or girl, Mom and Dad would not have fought so much and so might still be together.

Ridiculous?

Yes. But we are dealing with a four-or five-year-old mind here. We often make the mistake of assuming that children will understand what we are telling them because it seems so simple to *us.* But it is not. They need to be told that *nothing* they did caused the divorce and nothing they do can reverse

146

the divorce. You can expect to have to repeat this again and again with young children before they will believe it.

In terms of school behavior, we know that children whose parents divorce during their preschool years are much more likely to have trouble with fighting and other forms of aggression at school. They will also probably have trouble staying with an assignment until it is finished, and will have poorer overall adjustment to school. Dependency needs also surface in these children and some will develop into "clingers" with teachers, fishing for compliments and reassurances that they are doing right.

Five to Six Years

A study done in 1984 found that children who were under six when parents divorced were three times as likely to need psychological help than other children. These problems have the same cause as those we have already examined, but they show up differently.

Aggressive behavior tends to become a problem, especially with boys in this age group, when the father leaves the home. This is caused primarily by the loss of security felt by these youngsters. Observable anxiety expresses itself in trouble sleeping, fears of being alone, being left at the store or shopping mall, and a general irritability. Along with the anxiety, parents are likely to see whining and tantrum behavior, moodiness, restlessness, and, occasionally, eating disorders. As was true with preschool aged children, primary level teachers always know within a few days of school which children have experienced the divorce of their parents.

The prime cause of all of these disorders in previously normal children stems from their sense of being rejected by the parent who left and concerns over whether the separation is permanent. The remaining parent can minimize the difficulties and retain power and influence by reassuring children that the divorce *is* final, will not be changed by *anything* they do, was not their fault, and that the absent parent still loves and cares for them and will continue to see them and be involved in their lives.

The importance of repeated reassurances that the family

147

will continue even under changed circumstances cannot be emphasized too much. The uncertainty will diminish gradually, but remember that divorce is a time-limited problem for children. Parents have every reasonable expectation that the situation will improve *if* the parent does not surrender their power in the home and start giving in to the children in order to win their love. Parental guilt is the main thing that needs to be controlled if we are to keep the remaining family together with a minimum of difficutly.

Seven to Eight Years

Major changes in the ability to understand takes place in this age bracket as children move to what Jean Piaget[1] called "concrete operations thought."

By age seven a normal child can understand the concept of "forever." Along with the ability to grasp the permanence of a divorce, children also develop an awareness of death in a new way. They often become interested in the death of pets or people they know. It is important that a parent explain the concept of Heaven (minimizing hell at this age). Children must be helped to feel secure in the idea that God loves them individually and will care for them. Children can have some of their security needs met by being told and taught about a loving God who loves them even more than parents.

Because they are able to grasp the concept of permanent changes in their young lives, children of divorce can be expected to have some loyalty conflicts over which parent they are expected to love more. The custodial parent needs to help the children understand that it is all right to have these feelings about parents. As long as parents do not use the kids as a conduit for messages of hostility like, "ask your father why the support payment is late," or "go back and tell your mother that I'll send the money when I can," children will adjust to the changes.

Mothers seem to have a special problem with their sons on the issue of loyalty. Moms need to understand that the man she was once married to is still important to her sons *and* daughters, but male children especially need to continue to have an adult male model available to them. Dad is still a hero in the eyes of a boy, no matter what he may have done to create problems for Mom. He must not have his character assassinated in front of the children. Mom's anger may be justified, but the children should not be asked to share it.

Depending on the length of time since the divorce, children may go through a period of wishing for reconciliation and working to achieve it. It is not surprising if the children start asking questions about the permanency of the break-up. Assuming that reconciliation is not possible, the custodial or resident parent needs to express this to the kids so that they will not "work" to get Mom and Dad back together.

At this age, children can be expected to understand that both parents are good people who just can't live together anymore. The rule of explanation is to keep it simple, remembering that we are dealing with a child's mind and a child's understanding. Tell them what they need to know, and don't expand unnecessarily.

The problems common to children of divorce at this age include excessive restlessness, obstinancy and disobedience, classroom misbehavior, and impulsiveness. All these problems are more obvious and frequent in boys and can be met with calm reassurances that everything will eventually be all right. Mothers help by reinforcing their determination to lead the family and by showing strength as well as love when dealing with disobedience and other problems.

Nine to Twelve Years

As growth into the "tween-age" years occurs, expecting responsible behavior and providing opportunities to be responsible helps with adjustment. Babysitting and household chores tell children that Mom trusts them and feels they can help.

Sometimes we see "parentification" developing. When a child begins to take on the role of parent, especially with younger children, the resident parent must confront that child and give them permission to continue to be a child. Children feel guilty about divorce, too, and they will often try to reduce their guilt by being perfect and by helping more than they should. Piaget also said that play is the work of children, and there is no advantage in letting children grow up too fast.

Parents will sometimes inadvertently encourage this parentification by unburdening themselves about their problems to the oldest child. This is never good and should be avoided at all costs. We must not use the children as friends and age-mates. They cannot handle it no matter how mature they seem to be.

Another aspect of parentification is a form of false maturity wherein a child begins to act like a grown-up, even to the point of trying to tell Mom what she should do. When this happens, we can expect that child to eventually develop problems with psychosomatic illness, depression, and anger. Even though the child wants to help, they will not be able to bear up under the pressure of adult problems.

Clearly, children are helped most in post-divorce adjustment by a parent who is confident of her parenting skills, willing to bear her emotional burdens without involving the children, and powerful enough to enforce house rules. Discipline breeds security in this or any age group.

Adolescence

There is a split decision on which age is most traumatic when parents divorce. Many experts believe adolescents experience the greatest difficulty in accepting a divorce but have different, and less obvious, ways of showing it. Again we need to remember that in our culture, adolescence usually begins with puberty and ends with financial independence.

The major differences between adolescents and their younger siblings relates to the movement into adult thought beginning around 12 or 13 coupled with their rising self-centeredness. Even in families not experiencing divorce, we can expect a young adolescent to be less sympathetic to parents' problems than the younger kids because of their own concerns. Older teens are concerned about their parents' separating, but deal with it differently because they have their own anxieties to face.

When a teenager is told of the finality of a divorce, several

150

things are likely to happen. Parents need to be aware of these things and recognize them as a reaction to the divorce, not a problem in the adolescent. For example, most teens will withdraw from a family undergoing marital stress. This is done because of their sense of helplessness and their desire to avoid the pain that comes with involvement. The younger the adolescent, the greater the withdrawal, especially in boys. This usually takes the form of physical withdrawal to their rooms. their music, or their friends—anything to escape the emotional stress of the fighting between Mom and Dad. When there is severe tension between the two people they love most, sometimes the only way to handle it is to withdraw. Some may even withdraw to a fantasy world of their own creation; others withdraw emotionally.

Because adolescents tend to make value judgments on an absolute basis, loyalty issues become a major problem. Teens will not readily accept the notion that both parents are equally responsible and will quickly take sides with one or the other, often on the basis of sex. Teenagers will express anger with greater intensity toward the parent who was most valued before the divorce. Because of this, parents will want to protect teens from sharing unnecessarily in their own anger.

If it is the father who leaves the home, which is almost always true, boys have difficulty with loyalty and girls have difficulty dealing with what is often taken as sexual rejection. Not that Dad was doing anything wrong with the girls, but teenage girls often have crushes on Dad. They fantasize about dating and marrying someone just like him. When he leaves the family, she can feel deserted in almost the same way as her mother.

As we stated in earlier chapters, parents need to be careful to maintain previous discipline standards. They must not allow teenagers to manipulate them because of guilt over the divorce. We will deal with this issue again when we look at discipline in detail.

The self-esteem of teenagers declines following a divorce until about age 18 or so, and then it begins to rise again. One way teens may react to this decline is with alterations in their maturity. We have seen examples of hypermaturity, moving into adulthood too soon, and wanting privileges not appropriate for their age. We have also seen teens who did not want to grow up and acted younger than they should.

Teenagers who act out their feelings and get into trouble are usually hypermature and frequently get involved in drugs, alcohol, or sex. We need to be aware that a basic need of teens is for help in controlling themselves. We should not be reluctant to insist on them living within the rules even after a divorce.

Summary of The Thoughts and Feelings of Children of Divorce

Children go through a predictable series of thoughts and feelings as they are forced to confront the divorce of their parents. These reactions reflect the insecurities and sense of abandonment that nearly always follow divorce and provide the main challenges for parents who wish to minimize that impact. I will list them and make a brief comment on each regarding how a parent might try to help a child or teenager adjust.

Anger. Normal reactions of children to divorce include anger. This is an extreme sense of frustration over a situation that is terribly important to them but over which they seem to have no control. Parents can help by explaining the irreversibility of their decision to dissolve the marriage and by giving the child permission to feel angry. Recognize the emotion when it is seen, legitimize it for the child by telling him it is okay to feel that way, and then model a lack of anger in your own life.

Loss. Many children go through a mourning process similar to what occurs when a loved one dies. Parents report denial in children when they first learn of the divorce, then a period of anger and resentment toward both parents, bargaining with parents to see if there isn't some way to bring them back together, then depression when nothing has worked, and, finally, acceptance. This may or may not occur in a given family depending on the ages of the children involved, what the marriage was like prior to the divorce, and how the custody and visitation arrangements are structured.

Abandonment. Young children fear abandonment more than death. They know what it feels like to be lost, while death is beyond the understanding of most younger children. Again, security is the issue. Parents can greatly reduce the trauma by providing calm, consistent reassurances that both parents will remain with the child, though under different circumstances.

Blaming the Parent. One parent will always be singled out as the "prime mover" in a divorce. Even when children know that one parent was the cause of the divorce, the custodial parent is usually the recipient of blame for what the child perceives as "forcing" the issue. This will pass if Mom does not defend herself to the child. Children place responsibility for a divorce on the most guilty parent, but if the other parent simply does not respond, this criticism slowly dissipates.

Blaming Self. Most children of divorce spend a lot of time and energy trying to figure out if they were somehow responsible for the divorce. Usually, they come to the conclusion that they were, at least in part. This issue of responsibility is greater with children between school age and adolescence. Help can be provided by asking a child what is on his or her mind and discussing the issues in an almost adult manner when he acts depressed. Children do not enjoy this feeling, and it won't take too much effort by the parent to convince them that they are wrong.

Immaturity. There is a natural tendency in human beings to regress when under severe pressure. Many four-and five-year-old children "forget" their toilet training when a divorce occurs. There may be a return to tantrum behavior, whining, and even baby-talk. These behaviors are based in the sense of insecurity felt by children after a parent has left the home, but they will diminish as the child has that security re-established

153

by the remaining parent. This is usually accomplished through consistent reassurances that everything is all right and that nothing is going to happen to cause the live-in parent to leave them.

Hypermaturity. Some children seem to reason that if one parent has left home, and there is nothing they can do about it, that they will fill the void and become a parent-substitute in the home. Girls seem to do this more than boys. The pattern begins with requests to be allowed to help which gradually escalates into the child becoming a pseudo-parent. One of the few benefits that come to children whose parents have divorced is greater maturity. The negative side to this is that it can grow to the point where the child is no longer a child, does not play or have much fun, is overly serious about everything, and begins trying to control the parent. A serious talk between Mom and child about who is in control of the situation will usually be enough to give the child permission to be a child again.

Reconciliation Preoccupation. When children get to the pre-teen stage, we often see a rebirth of the belief that maybe there *is* something they can do to bring Mom and Dad back together again. This seems to be a recognition that it is probably now or never, and they want to take one more shot at healing the family. If a remarriage has occurred for either parent, this will not take place.

Self-Esteem. Children have their existence based in their family. When one-half of their parent support goes to live elsewhere after a divorce, they take on some of the blame and guilt. Self-esteem goes through the floor. Kids are embarrassed to have parents who have divorced. They don't know that about half of any elementary school class will also be from divorced homes because they tend to avoid letting others know what has happened to them. Parents and teachers can help by letting the child know how common an occurrence this is and how well other kids have adjusted to it in time.

154

Sex-Role Identity. Ninety-two percent of divorced children live with Mother. This is much more of a problem for boys than girls in that not only has one parent left the home, but it was the parent boys need to learn a sex-role. Obviously, the age of the boy at the time of the divorce makes a difference in this regard. For families where the mother does not remarry within five years, a divorce has the greatest sexual impact on boys between four and eight. However, others can help make up for the absence of father. Uncles, a grandfather, even a male teacher, or Boy Scout leader can greatly reduce the tendency toward effeminacy in this age group. Mothers need to be very careful about their comments regarding their ex-husband and males in general following a divorce. Strong feelings are to be expected, but the children should not be allowed to participate in them.

Devaluation. There is likely to be an overall decline in the self-concept and sense of self-worth in children after a divorce. Depression, anger, and self-esteem problems result from the realization that life has been permanently altered by events totally beyond their control. The thinking goes, "I am simply not worth as much as a person now as I was before my parents split up, and there is nothing I can do about it!" When a parent sees this happening, the key is to get counseling for the child and provide activities that are fun and rewarding. Children are very resilient if we allow them the opportunity.

Finally, the controlling element in whether a child makes a good adjustment or a poor adjustment to a divorce, depends primarily on the custodial parent. Parental attitudes about life, the ex-spouse, family responsibilities, children, work, and everything else connected to the trauma of going through a divorce are all factors that control the child's adaptation. If we do not put roadblocks in their path, they will bounce back. If we provide security when they need it, including firm discipline, they will feel reassured knowing that Mom *is* still in charge. If Mom and Dad do not use the children as instruments of war with each other, the children will have

155

only a minimal amount of emotional upset. Both parents must contribute to this sense of security, but for obvious reasons of time and proximity, the custodial parent bears the primary responsibility.

Single Parenting

Considering the comments I receive from parents about the difficulties involved in being a single parent, I wonder if a divorcing couple wouldn't rather bite the bullet and stay together in spite of their difficulties. I have counseled many fathers who lost custody *and* contact with their children in the years since their divorce and felt terribly cheated and guilty. Many single-again mothers with custody of their children have told me they would not do it again, knowing what they know now.

Single parenting is difficult under the best of circumstances, and we almost never have the best of circumstances. Researchers estimate that by 1990 one of every three children under age 18 will be living with only one parent, and living with a mother or father trying to raise them virtually alone.

What makes single parenting so difficult?

To begin with, it is exhausting. One parent now must do the work previously done by two, and on just one paycheck. Our entire social structure is built around a two-parent system. Though the rising divorce rate may force some adjustments to be made, right now schools almost always send letters home addressed to "Mr. & Mrs." When teachers talk to students, they always refer to parents (plural).

Single parenting limits the family's ability to solve problems, two heads being better than one after all. Emotional support is also bound to be diminished. Even though there might not have been much before, there was probably *some* support. When problems of a sexual nature come up, questions about dating, or concern over acceptable behavior with the opposite sex, one of the opposite sex parents is missing.

Single parents often experience loneliness and guilt. The loneliness can lead to a too intense emotional relationship between Mom and the kids. The danger is that Mom will get

156

too much emotional support and be reluctant to let go when the kids need to get out with their own friends. This is the "smother love" we discussed in an earlier chapter.

The single parent, usually the custodial parent, will be called on to deal with childhood difficulties created or worsened by the divorce. Common among such problems are school phobias, excessive and unreasonable fear over the possible death or injury to the remaining parent, and an excessive sense of responsibility. When problems of obedience occur, single parents show a strong tendency to become either excessively strict or too lenient.

Are there benefits to single parenting?

Yes, but they are frequently offset by the disadvantages.

Benefits of single parenting include the children growing closer to mother, accepting more responsibility, showing greater maturity, relying on friends for social support, and sometimes becoming even closer to the absent father.

The disadvantages are obvious, but can be summed up as follows.

Children may lose contact and become detached from their absent parent. Often the family has to move to an apartment after living in a single family home. There are new requirements for helping with housework, and the extra responsibility is not always warmly received by the kids. Moving to another area may be required, forcing children to lose their sense of support from friends and familiarity with their surroundings.

Benefits and disadvantages aside, when God's plan for the family is disrupted, problems are to be expected. How any given child will adjust to that disruption depends on the facts we have already mentioned. But one thing is certain, there *will* be more problems after the divorce than before!

What About Remarriage?

The majority of second marriages produce good results. The statistics vary, but most stepfamily situations are bettter than single-parenting. The issue is preparation. Knowing what to expect allows parents to prepare for the inevitable adjustment difficulties of a reconstituted family.

157

Preparation for parents involves recognizing that some problems need to be solved before the marriage takes place. Other problems need to be anticipated following the marriage. A list of the things to be resolved before the marriage includes:

1. Discipline and home rules. These must be agreed to by both primary parties to the marriage, as well as children, before going ahead with the marriage. It is true that children and teens may try to sabotage the marriage by not cooperating, but it is still desirable to deal with such issues before rather than after.

2. Division of labor at home. This means defining who will do what and for how long. It is an advantage to have a home populated by more people than before, but if there is no agreement beforehand about who does what, chaos will inevitably result.

3. Attitudes toward sex and sexual modesty. Combining families and children, which is usually the case with remarriages, involves putting children of different ages and sexes together in the same home, a challenge of adjustment under the best of circumstances. Reminders about closing bathroom doors and wearing a bathrobe in the morning are usually needed. If there are teenagers or preteens involved, parents need to discuss with each other and with the individual kids what is acceptable and what is required in the way of expressing emotions. It is sadly common that in families involving teenage or preteen girls, sexual manipulation by the stepfather is a frequent problem.

4. Eating habits. Mealtimes are a basic family process in most families. It is the time when we talk about our day and ask others about theirs. Meal preparation is an issue when Mom works outside the home. Even though this seems mundane, it is one of the main causes of serious arguments in reconstituted families. Decide on who will help, when, to what extent and be careful to lovingly enforce these decisions equitably.

158

5. Manners. If one side of the family has raised the children to say "yes, sir," "no, sir," and the other side has not, some adjustments need to be made ahead of time. What usually happens is that the new parents simply agree to accept what was done before, leading to a gradual diminishing of the more formal behavior. It seems that manners, like water, always seek the lowest level.

6. Moral and religious issues. Love is great, but things like which church the new family attends and what moral standards are expected must be addressed. These issues should be resolved with all family members before marriage. Clearly express what you believe, why you believe it, and how these issues will affect all the members of the family. If you can clearly explain these issues and discuss them openly, usually children will not be hesistant later to bring their questions to you. Honest, open communication will go a long way toward building trust.

7. Expression of negative emotions. The prospective new parents need to talk over their children's emotional tendencies and how each has dealt with them in the past. *What will we do when a child throws a tantrum? Will Dad or Mom deal with disobedience? What will be expected from each child when given instructions to do something?* The stepparent will have difficulty disciplining stepchildren in the beginning. Decide before marriage on discipline and then support each other. Do not let children play one against the other.

A stepfamily can be a great improvement over single-parenting. While we are not debating the theology of divorce and remarriage, we are acknowledging the fact that divorce does happen. Like any other sin, divorce is forgivable by God and restoration a matter to be dealt with between the Christian and the Lord. Where two believers find God's blessing for remarriage, we would encourage it. Much more could be said on this subject, but I will only emphasize again the great importance of parents showing a united front to their children, even in stepfamilies. There are bound to be disagreements. Parents can reduce this turmoil in the home by promising each other that they will not disagree about the children in front of the children and will settle all disputes on this subject behind closed doors. Children *must* see two united parents if the stepfamily is to survive. The ideal of a shared partnership of parents set forth by God is just as applicable for a reconstituted family as for an original family.

Parent unity *is* power!

Concluding Thoughts

God has ordained one man for one woman for one lifetime, but many of us, in this as in other areas of life, choose to do something other than what God would choose for us. Eventually, we pay the price for our rebellion.

Some are victims of the sins of others, doing everything we know to do to keep a marriage together, but without success. Some initiate the sin, willfully choosing, like Adam and Eve, to disobey God.

Because we believe God is a God of the second chance, and His forgiveness total, most of us are encouraged when we see a single-parent family overcoming the obstacles and honoring God in spite of difficulties. Yet the major danger threatening single parents or stepparents is the loss of power. Many things can drain our power and influence away from our children, but nothing creates a power outage like divorce. Power must be guarded when the family is under stress. Guarded so that it is not squandered by careless over-application or lost through disuse.

Remember, nothing shows love to our children as clearly as parent power. We know that God loves us too much to allow more to happen than we can bear (I Corinthians 10:13), and we know that God is too *powerful* to let something happen that would be too much for us (Jeremiah 32:17-19, 27).

Love and power. These are the elements most needed in single-parenting and stepparenting. One without the other will result in continuing problems and family unhappiness.

FOOTNOTES:
[1]Piaget, Jean and Inhelder, B., *Psychology of the Child* 1969, Basic Books, NY, NY.

9
POWER DISCIPLINE

Children and teenagers cannot learn to be disciples without first learning discipline. Counselors who work with Christian families generally agree that nothing is in such short supply as effective discipline. Love is important, of course, as is unconditional acceptance and a positive and optimistic attitude about children. But there are many people in prison today, on drugs or alcohol, or involved in sexual immorality who were well loved as children. The absence of love can destroy a child, but the presence of love alone will not be enough.

Children need love *and* discipline.

Children and teenagers need to see a love from parents that is *powerful* enough to help them when they need it. They need a love strong enough to say no. (Much like God's.) They need a love that says, "I love you too much to stand by and watch you hurt yourself." They need a love that is powerful!

Chris—The Tantrum Artist

Mr. and Mrs. Wallace drove almost two hours to get to our counseling center; there just wasn't the help they needed in the small farming community where they lived. The appointment had been on my schedule for two weeks, and I wondered what kind of problem would motivate these parents to make a four hour round-trip drive to get some help.

I always want to talk with both parents before seeing their child, and usually this means a second appointment later in the week for the child. But because they had driven so far, we scheduled back-to-back sessions so I could see their son the same day.

The Wallaces seemed to be a normal enough Christian couple. Bob was a farm extension agent in their rural county,

161

and his wife Elaine stayed at home to care for eleven-year-old Chris and his nine-year-old sister April. Bob was a big man, looked like a farmer, and seemed unlikely to be a father who would have trouble controlling children. Elaine was much smaller than her husband and seemed the more upset of the two about their son's behavior.

Chris, I was told, had always been a difficult child to raise. He was explosive and impulsive; he acted spoiled though his parents denied overindulging him, but he did *not* get into trouble in school. Chris was a B to C student in the sixth grade. He was described as a quiet boy who was reasonably well liked by his teachers and had about average popularity with the other kids.

However, according to his parents, Chris had become a monster at home.

Over the last two years there had been a serious deterioration in Chris's behavior. He had kicked a hole in his bedroom wall after being scolded about talking back to his mother. He had jumped on his sister April's toys, trying to break them following an argument. He was more and more rebellious and disobedient. The final straw occurred when, in a fit of anger, he hit his mother with a closed fist, knocking her down and breaking her glasses.

Mrs. Wallace said that Chris was now too big to be physically controlled when Bob was not home, and talking to him seemed to do no good at all. Bob had spanked Chris without effect, and said that the effort of wrestling his son to be able to spank him was almost more than he could do. Privileges had been removed. The television set had been taken out of his bedroom for a period of weeks, and he was not allowed to spend the night or have friends over when he was misbehaving.

But Chris's behavior continued to worsen. His parents were beginning to think that Chris was headed for very serious trouble down the road unless something changed drastically. From what they had told me, I agreed.

As Bob and Elaine went out into the waiting room, I brought Chris inside so we could talk alone. This eleven-year-old was bright-eyed, alert, overweight, and exhibited an emotional maturity level that appeared to lag behind his intelligence. In other words, Chris talked older than he acted.

He admitted that what his parents had said was true, but blamed his parents and circumstances for the outbursts, something that confirmed his maturity level. Yes, he had done those things, including hit his mother, but he didn't mean to do them, "if only *she* would leave him alone." This idea of others causing his misbehavior ran consistently throughout our first meeting.

This boy had been able to manipulate his parents with increasing success. Now I had to try and help them figure out what to do about it. This set of parents was losing control in their home and had no idea what to do about it. Chris had developed his tantrum behavior into an art form. Discipline was not working.

How could I help Bob and Elaine with their son?

What did they need to know about discipline that could turn things around with their son?

I decided to begin with some basic principles of effective and powerful discipline.

Six Rules For Powerful Discipline

1. *Avoid Inadequate Methods.* When parents discipline, it is always with the hope that it won't be necessary next time. Whatever method is used, whether spanking, scolding, loss of privileges, or going to bed early, make sure the method is powerful enough to discourage the child from repeating the misbehavior.

Chris had a problem with hitting. He seemed to have a special preference for hitting his sister April at the slightest provocation. Dad would intervene, take Chris into his room and spank him, warn him not to hit April again, and the next day it *would* happen again.

What was wrong with Chris?

Was he so devoid of conscience and the ability to learn from mistakes that he was hopeless?

No, Chris wasn't any of these things. He was just a boy who didn't like his sister very much and got joy from punching her occasionally. There were times when he was *willing to pay the price* for the pure fun of smacking her one!

Bob wanted to know why the spankings didn't work. Surely Chris didn't enjoy the spanking; he fought it hard enough!

What Bob needed to know was that the spanking either wasn't hard enough, *or* it was just the wrong method to use with Chris. He needed to increase the power behind the physical methods or forget about spanking altogether and remove privileges, increasing the cost to Chris for his bad behavior.

Our son Doug didn't feel pain like most children. He could have a tooth filled with very little novocaine. Doug didn't feel a spanking very much either, so it was not effective. But take away his baseball glove for two days, and he would do *anything* we asked to get it back.

Bob Wallace needed to change his method of disciplining Chris. He needed to spank more and harder, or he needed to stop spanking for awhile and try some other methods. Power and flexibility were needed in the Wallaces in order to find the key to helping Chris learn to behave.

2. *Apply Discipline Immediately.* A basic rule of learning says that the shorter the time between an act and its consequences, the stronger will be the learning.

At times, Chris was allowed to escape punishment because his mother wanted to wait until Bob came home. Sometimes this cannot be avoided, and this was true with Chris. He *was* too big to be manhandled by his mom, and because he would not submit to her authority, she had to wait.

But sometimes Chris got out of it even when Bob was home. When Bob was working outside in the garden or on the truck, Chris knew he could disobey and his dad would not want to be called in to deal with it.

We worked out an arrangement so that Bob agreed to come in and deal with Chris immediately when called. Because of the seriousness of Chris's behavior, Bob also agreed to come

164

home when paged on his beeper while at work. This was a temporary arrangement designed to last only until they got the situation back under control. But it was an important step.

Chris had an absolute need to experience a powerful father immediately after a serious misbehavior. Kids will try *anything* to get a parent to postpone discipline. They know from experience that we don't like punishing children, and we are likely to forget. Forgetting encourages continued misbehavior.

3. *Be Reasonable and Flexible.* Most parents I have dealt with on disciplinary matters needed help to *moderate* their punishment methods. Many were heading for problems with the child abuse laws or just creating bitterness in their children for being so unreasonable. They needed help to calm down and be more thoughtful and controlled when correcting their children.

Not so with Bob Wallace!

Bob needed help to toughen up with Chris. I had a hard time understanding how Bob could be so calm about his wife getting hit in the face and her glasses broken by their own son. It turned out that Bob wasn't as calm as he first appeared, but he had learned to make it look that way because he did not know what to do with Chris.

I told Bob that he needed to make a distinction between intentional disobedience and the unintentional, emotional disobedience that all children are prone to do. He needed to tailor his discipline to fit Chris's age, level of understanding, number of warnings and prior offenses, and the intention to do wrong. Bob was to trust the Holy Spirit to give him discernment in deciding these things, and he didn't need any experts to tell him why his son of eleven-and-a-half years was doing what he was doing. The only experts on Chris were his parents, and they needed to remind themselves of this.

Bob and I talked about Chris and decided that Chris knew he was loved, but did not know he was loved enough to be controlled. I told Bob and Elaine that God had given them this child to raise, and He expected them to be the authorities

165

about Chris's motivations. I could help with discipline ideas, but only they knew what their son was really like.

4. *Require an Incompatible Response.* When possible, Bob needed to make sure that Chris fixed what he broke during his tantrums. If Chris broke a lamp in his room and it could not be repaired, he would just have to live without a lamp. If he kicked a hole in his wall, he could either help Dad fix it, or go without dessert for a month. If he hit his sister again, he would be punished and be required to apologize (yes, *required* to apologize to her), and to ask her forgiveness.

Children and adolescents made to clean up what they mess up and fix what they damage usually do not repeat the misbehavior. Taking a spanking or enduring loss of privileges is one thing, but having to spend hours gluing a lamp back together or plastering over a hole in a bedroom wall is something else again. Fixing what you do wrong is *embarrassing!*

5. *Avoid Rewards After Punishment.* It sounds strange, I know, but many parents feel the need to apologize when they discipline their children. So many parents have bought the world's message about the dangers of exhibiting a godly power and influence in the home that when we do administer a spanking or something, we feel guilty. Because *we* feel bad, we apologize, take the child out for a treat, and generally confuse his immature mind.

Think what it sounds like to an eight-year-old to hear Dad say, "Son, I'm really sorry I had to give you that spanking, but well, I just *had* to. I sure don't like doing that, and I hope you won't make it necessary for me to do it again. Everything all right now, son?"

The eight-year-old is thinking, "Dad didn't want to do it. I didn't want the spanking. So why did I get spanked? And why is Dad apologizing if he really believes he did the right thing? This sure is confusing!"

It *is* confusing, and completely unbiblical. Can you find any examples in the Bible where Jehovah God apologized when He delivered punishment to a person or nation?

Nowhere are there examples of God saying He is sorry for doing what He warned He would do if the sin continued. Apologizing to an immature mind is the same as saying it should not have happened. Adults know what we mean when we say we are sorry the spanking had to be given, but children do not comprehend that perspective.

When punishment is given, that's it! No apologies, no ice cream, no trips to the toy store. Let the lesson sink in, and you won't have to repeat it. This is what happened with Chris. His dad would feel guilty for the little punishment he gave, and, in order to make the family happy again, they would all go out for ice cream.

Avoid rewards after punishment!

6. *Make Sure the Behavior is Correctible.* Are there children who can't help getting in trouble? Of course there are. Some are hyperactive. Some learning disabled or emotionally disturbed. Some have problems they were born with that we can't yet understand. One of our children was hyperactive, and until the thirteenth year, this kid was really something.

But not so with Chris. He had none of these problems. He was just poorly trained. But with a lot of effort and godly power, Mr. and Mrs. Wallace were able to show Chris some tough love. The last I heard, his home behavior was much closer to his school behavior. Chris learned that his parents, and especially his dad, *could* love him enough to help him stay out of trouble. Children need limits to feel loved (Deuteronomy 8:5; Proverbs 19:18).

Why Punishment May Not Work

Sometimes God needs to teach us something that we don't want to learn. If we resist Him long enough, He may allow sickness or injury to come into our lives so that He can speak to us while we are paying attention. But once the learning is accomplished, we move on. The chastening of God is for a specific purpose and the emphasis is always on teaching, never on simple retribution. Never does God try to "just get even with us" (Hebrews 12:5-11).

When we use punishment to correct and teach our children, it should always be the last resort, used when all other attempts to get a child's attention have failed. But sometimes even a last resort like spanking or some other form of punishment still doesn't work. What then?

What can parents do when everything has failed, and the child or teenager continues to disobey and rebel?

When a method isn't working, change it, strengthen it, or forget it. But don't continue doing something the same way in the hope that the message will eventually get through. We may think we have tried everything, but I have yet to meet a basically normal child or teenager who could not be reached with some method of discipline. If experts have any value to parents like the Wallaces, it is in suggesting some things they had not thought of yet.

When parents over-rely on one form of discipline, especially a physical method like spanking, they frequently get opposite results from what they hoped. Children often continue their bad behavior in spite of the strongest physical methods possible. I have known children who were on the brink of being classified as abused but who continued in their rebellion and misbehavior in spite of severe punishment. There are several reasons why over-reliance on physical methods is bad for children.

For example, extensive punishment may set up a series of escape responses in children that could be more harmful than the behavior for which they were being punished. A child may come to fear Dad and the belt more than he fears doing wrong. So he behaves solely to escape physical pain. The problem is what happens when Dad and the belt are no longer around. If getting spanked is the only thing discouraging bad behavior, not conscience or guilt, when the spanking ends, bad behavior will resume.

Extensive reliance on physical punishment also creates problems by creating emotional reactions in children. Children can become so anxious about the spanking that impulsive behaviors like running away or striking back may occur. The biblical idea of "not provoking children to wrath" is important here (Ephesians 6:4). The pain that goes along with physical punishment may be so terrifying to a child, that he or she will do anything to escape it, including hitting back.

Punishment can also have an impact on parents. No healthy-minded parent enjoys punishing children. When we believe, usually at the urging of some self-proclaimed expert, that spanking is the *only* biblical method, we set ourselves up for some genuine guilt. We will feel guilty and in error when we go too far with punishment. This guilt can make us feel anxious and sad much of the time and so have an impact on the non-misbehaving members of the family.

While physical punishment does work to stop bad behavior, experience has shown that it will reappear shortly after the punishment has stopped. Simple punishment, such as a spanking, will not eliminate a child's motivation for doing wrong. So, when an opportunity presents itself, the behavior happens again. For punishment to be as effective as we would like, the bad behavior would have to be punished *every* time it occurs, which is, of course, impossible.

Punishments also lose their effectiveness with overuse, leading to a gradual increase in the severity level of the punishment, which often leads to injuries and accusations of child abuse. Remember that the most common cause for parents abusing their children is an over-dependence on physical methods of discipline and a lack of knowledge of other methods that *do* work as well or better.

Parents who rely on physical methods alone to control children are setting an example for them, an example of force and aggression as an acceptable way of solving problems. Bullies in school *always* come from homes where Dad is quick to use the belt. This is what they learn; this is what they practice as they grow, and this is what they will do to their children.

Finally, parents who over-use spankings and beatings to discipline children become less effective as parents over time. This occurs because their value as a provider of love and other forms of positive reinforcement decreases because they are so often associated with pain. Children will eventually become "flinchy" around the punishing parent and that parent will be avoided, even when things are okay. We also know that the person in the family who gives out the most punishment receives the most punishment, not physical necessarily, but by being ignored, disliked, and feared.

My Friend Jerry

Jerry is dead now, killed in a head-on collision with a tree about fifteen years ago. I visited his family at the funeral, and I have never seen such grief.

Jerry was a strange kid, as I look back on the years of our growing up together. His dad was an absolute tyrant in the home, drank heavily, and was frightening to all of us kids in the neighborhood. None of us could imagine what it would be like to have a father like Jerry's dad.

Trouble was a big part of Jerry's life. In school and at home, he was *always* getting into trouble for something, and many of those childhood adventures included me.

One experience came back to me as I stood next to Jerry's body in the funeral home. There was a time when all of our parents were called out in the middle of the night to come to the police station to pick us up. We had snuck out of our bedrooms and met for a little running around late at night. We were all scared of what our parents would do, but Jerry's reaction was different. Even at eleven-years-old, I could tell that the fear in his eyes was different. When Jerry's dad came in, he started to cry, something our gang *never* did, and he totally lost control. All this at the sight of his father.

We were sent home and punished of course, as we should have been. But we didn't see Jerry for a few days. When he came back to school, he looked like he had been beaten up, which, of course, he had.

Jerry's life continued to be unpleasant. He quit high school, joined the service, began to drink we were told, and then came the accident when he was about twenty-three.

All his life Jerry had been severely punished for mis-behavior. The more he was punished, the more he determined to make life miserable for his father. In Jerry's life, punishment *encouraged* bad behavior because it was not

170

given with love. He and I had long talks in those days, and I know that if his dad had eased up on the spankings and beatings and shown some love, Jerry would have been very different. He might even be alive today.

I think Jerry killed himself that day when he hit the tree. I think that his death was Jerry's final way of making life miserable for the father who beat him.

And I think it worked. At the funeral home that day, and later at the cemetery, Jerry's dad was the saddest human being I have ever seen. I have never seen such grief, and because I was Jerry's best friend during those growing up years, I know that the grief was really guilt, self-blame that Jerry's dad would carry with him forever.

And it was so unnecessary. Just a little love mixed in with discipline would have spared that family a lifetime of sadness and guilt. I hope I never meet another family like Jerry's. But knowing that family made a lasting impression on me.

Disciplining Adolescents

Should teenagers be spanked?

I am asked that question almost as often as any other when I meet with parents to discuss adolescence. Their questions about this subject are heartfelt. Most really want to know how to help teenagers control their behavior, but are confused because of the different messages Christians get from different sources.

The major point we covered in an earlier chapter is that adolescence is not a concept existent during Bible times. Adolescence was created at the beginning of this century in response to changes in American society. We know that according to Jewish tradition, children become adults at age twelve or thirteen. A ceremony was conducted to mark the occasion, and often is even today.

When it comes to the issue of dealing with today's teens, we must apply those passages directed at dealing with people in general. Children constitute a separate category, as do young adults, adults, and older people. But there is no designation that can be stretched to fit what we think of adolescence today, not even young adults.

171

Consequently, we are left with the conclusion that there is no biblical permission for physical punishment of teenagers.

No Biblical Precedent

There are no examples of people in the age group we would call teenagers being physically punished by parents. Children are spanked in the Bible; teenagers are not. The Bar Mitzvah ceremony contains the words, "today you are a man," and while twelve-year-olds were not given all the privileges of adults, they are no longer treated as children.

I believe that God would have us know that today's teenagers are adults in the earliest stages of adulthood, not children in the last stages of childhood.

Because of this emerging adulthood, spanking or beating teenagers *never* works!

Spanking teens is humiliating and provokes them to wrath. Some teens will tolerate it for awhile out of love and respect for their Christian parents, but if it continues, it will always produce negative, counterproductive results. Always! Remember, God humbles us but does not humiliate us when we sin. It is an important principle of discipline to remember.

Disciplining adolescents requires a self-confidence in parents that will enable them to negotiate (not on doctrinal issues, of course) on issues of life not clearly spelled out in the Bible. In our family there is no negotiation on smoking or drinking, for example, but Linda and I would listen to an argument in favor of changing curfew for special occasions or for loosening the music code at home.

I have counseled with countless teenagers and college-aged young people still wrestling with ill feelings toward a parent who continued to spank into their teens. These kids love their parents and know that love is returned, but they carry the burden of trying to understand why their parents insisted on treating them like children when they called them young adults . . . and expected adult behavior.

I don't have an answer for them. The best I can do is to help them understand that their parents did love them and *thought*

172

they were doing the right thing.

On a "Focus on the Family" radio program, Dr. James Dobson said that spankings are one necessary aspect of teaching children right and wrong, but that spankings should diminish as the child gets older so that by the time teen years are begun, spankings will be a memory of childhood only. Parents with teens who need a spanking have already lost the battle. More spankings will only make things worse. It is my firm conviction that there is *no* biblical permission for spanking adolescents.

None!

What the Bible Says About Discipline and Punishment

The Bible is never a problem in and of itself. God's Word often presents challenges to those who seek truth in its revelation, to those willing to invest time and effort in an attempt to find the instructions contained in its pages, but never is the Bible the problem. Interpretations, translations, and revisions require careful study but the message is intact and complete regardless of the language used or liberal attempts at emasculating its power. The message of the Bible continues from generation to generation for those who have an ear to hear.

The challenge for Christian parents is to understand with discernment what the Bible does and does not say about the discipline and punishment of children. Child discipline is not a doctrinal issue like salvation or the virgin birth, but child discipline does impact daily family life and is, therefore, a critical subject in Christian parenting.

Why does there seem to be so much discussion among Christians about spanking, what kind of "rod" to use, should parents use a hand to spank, and should parents spank at all?

The reason child discipline is an issue today, as never before, is because so many Christian parents are poorly educated about the Bible. At the same time, we are bombarded daily with the media messages pushing the liberal agenda, and all this while the world continues to degenerate. This combina-

173

tion has led many Christian parents to accept a well-meant but incorrect idea of biblical discipline.

Many have lost their parent power and influence because they have overreacted to the degeneration we all see around us. We hear of robberies and murders in our schools, of rapes and assaults on teachers and students, of flagrant and open drug use with only the most feeble attempts at correction, and we become afraid for our children. We decided to start our own schools out of fear that there is nothing we can do to stop the tide that threatens to swallow our children in the public schools.

Unfortunately, many of us overreacted by establishing Christian schools with discipline systems second only to the Marine Corps. We instituted demerits and reprimands, suspensions and expulsions, and a generally grace-less system that alienated a good percentage of our kids. In spite of the fact that our kids were not the problem in the first place, we paddled children and adolescents alike. We used paddles, straps, boards, yardsticks, pointers, and just about anything else that could be derived loosely from the magic word "rod" found in several of the Proverbs, usually Proverbs 13:24.

And all the while grace and compassion were slowly disappearing beneath the sea of rules.

At home we reacted by becoming more authoritarian in hopes of guaranteeing that our kids would not turn into the wild-eyed freaks we saw on television. But many of us forgot about love at home just as we misplaced grace at school. We just overlooked the Holy Spirit, and we didn't follow the example of the Bereans in searching the Scriptures daily to see if those things we did were true and biblical.

Of course we loved our children, but love was often smothered by rules or disguised by legalism.

To be sure, there were many social developments that caused us to overreact. The Supreme Court decisions on abortion and school prayer were accurately seen as threats to the traditional family unit. We read of Sweden passing laws making spanking illegal and how some children were actually being encouraged by teachers to report parents who spanked them.

We watched and wondered if it could happen in our country. We forgot what Jesus said about obeying Caesar as long as Caesar did not conflict with God (Matthew 22:21), and some of us found ourselves in difficulty because we didn't know what the Bible said about God or Caesar. Our fear led to legalistic overreaction which in turn led to the surrendering of the power of the Holy Spirit in our role as parents.

The government began cracking down on child abuse, and some Christian parents began to wonder if spanking would get them into trouble with the law. We saw the horror stories of abused and battered children suffering terrible damage at the hands of their parents, and we wondered if we were capable of such things. We were offended and confused by newspaper stories about radical religious groups practicing the most brutal forms of punishment on children and teenagers and claiming to be following biblical dictates.

I attended a national convention on child abuse two years ago and saw the evidence that makes our officials worried. Child abuse in all its forms *is* on the increase. There is no doubt about it. What I was not prepared for was the apparently universal opinion among the experts there that *spanking* is a form of child abuse. I do not agree. But most of the experts there agreed, and they will be a force to be reckoned with in the days to come.

Is spanking child abuse?

Are these doctors and other experts correct?

Are Christian parents who spank their children violating the law?

The Bible tells us that physical methods of disciplining children are acceptable, but secular experts say no! Are parents who spank similar to child abusers? Is this one of those areas that will bring us into conflict with Caesar and lead us into civil disobedience?

In my opinion, no. Once we learn what the Bible *really* says about controlling and disciplining children, the problem vanishes. It is *only* when we are ignorant of God's Word or choose not to believe it, that we find ourselves in trouble.

Biblical discipline is always fair, reasonable, non-injurious, loving and forgiving.

175

Consider with me some common Bible passages related to the discipline of children.

> *Foolishness is bound in the heart of a child; but the rod of correction shall drive it far from him.* Proverbs 22:15

Should Christian parents assume this passage to be a guarantee that spanking with a rod will correct behavior? Can foolishness be controlled with the rod as an infection is controlled with antibiotics?

No, of course not!

A rod of correction was used in biblical times to beat unfaithful servants and to discipline children. But a rod was also used as a teaching instrument, just as today's teachers might use a pointer at the chalkboard. We can assume fairly that "the rod of correction" was, at times, nothing more than an instrument of teaching, never touching the child's body.

> *He that spareth his rod hateth his son: but he that loveth him chasteneth him betimes.* Proverbs 13:24

Betimes refers to each morning, or literally, with the dawn.

Are we to understand this verse as recommending a spanking every morning along with the oatmeal? I know some who believe this to be almost literally true!

But no. What this verse says is that a father who does not teach, instruct, and train his children does not love them (cf. Deuternonomy 6:1-9). In Bible times a rod served many purposes, including that of getting the attention of a daydreaming child.

We are to teach our children every day, not beat them every day. God is always fair and reasonable. He would never tolerate or require such abusive treatment of the children for whom His Son died.

But what about spanking itself?

Look at this passage from the book of Proverbs.

> *Withhold not correction from the child: for if thou beatest him with the rod, he shall not die. Thou shalt beat him with the rod, and shall deliver his soul from hell.* Proverbs 22:13-14

The promise here is that if parents spank a child with the correct kind of instrument, he will not be injured or killed. The word that has become "rod" in English is taken from a Hebrew word that means "branch of sapling tree," in other words, a switch.

God is telling parents that whatever the method of administering discipline, it must not be capable of injury or death. The switch is such an instrument, but the principle is more important than the specific word. We are instructed to do *nothing* that would hurt or injure our children. Children are loaned to us for a little season. They are a heritage of the Lord and belong to God (Psalm 127:3). He will not tolerate their being hurt. Remember what God said about those who exploit or injure His "little ones" (Matthew 18:6)? They would be better off if a millstone had been fastened around their necks, and they had been tossed into the depths of the sea.

We could go on at length about biblical discipline. It could fill hundreds of pages with no effort at all. But our point is simple. God will not have us injure or abuse the children He has loaned to us to raise. He expects us to be wise, good stewards of these treasures. A rod is a teaching and disciplining tool. It is to be flexible and incapable of doing serious harm, and the flat of the hand is not prohibited as an instrument of spanking. What we do, we do in love under the leading of the Holy Spirit, following biblical teachings.

Parents are to be models for their children and guides for their thoughts and behavior. We are to be judges and disciplinarians when needed, but we do what is necessary with grace, being imitators of God in His way of correcting *us*. We look to the Bible as the final authority, and when a specific answer is not provided, we ask for the guidance of the Holy Spirit, a privilege reserved to Christian parents.

Parent power in discipline comes from imitating God's love for His children to our children, and to be as merciful *and* as powerful as He is with us.

10
DEVOLOPING A POWERFUL MORALITY IN CHILDREN

Moral sensitivity must spring from something. Morality is not an inborn trait, nor is it something that can be forced on the unwilling. Morality is learned voluntarily, willingly, or it is not learned at all. Moral judgment and sensitivity are acquired over several years of being parented by adults holding moral values themselves. Once those moral values are internalized, they are never lost. Although fought against and rejected by some, moral teachings are never forgotten and remain an influence throughout life. Morality is acquired in the first years of life and remains powerful forever.

Power and Morality

Consider the power behind a "no." Such negative responses are a young child's first feeble attempts at establishing independence, a form of power. The terrible two's and three's are filled with no's because it is during these years a child tests limits and pushes for independence.

Think with me for a moment about the power behind a young person's ability to say no. There is, at present, an anti-drug campaign built around the idea of, "Just say no!" Why is it so hard to get people to say no? Is it harder to say no than yes? We would think so from the media messages we hear.

When a child, teenager, or adult says "no," it is usually a reaction to something they believe to be wrong. Not necessarily a sinful wrong, but perhaps just refusing that piece of chocolate cake. Sometimes it is a more serious no, as when a thirteen-year-old is invited to take an unknown pill or puff his first marijuana cigarette.

Being moral means having the strength, the power, to say "no." I know that there are times when the moral answer is

178

yes, as when we agree to contribute to feed the poor or to join an anti-pornography crusade, but most of the time the moral choice is the "no" choice.

So why is it so hard for people to say no? Every day thousands of people are becoming addicted to drugs and alcohol because they make the "yes" choice. Why is it so difficult for teenage girls to say "no" to the advances of a boyfriend and risk becoming pregnant and unmarried? Why is it so difficult for Christian men and women to say no to sexual advances and avoid the terrible damage we see being inflicted on our families?

The "no" choice is usually the hard choice when it comes to moral temptations. "Yes" is much easier, often much more fun for the short term, and eventually much more dangerous, especially to young people.

Christian parents need to see the power of morality. We need to model moral power in our own lives while we try to teach moral choices to our kids. We need to know that power and Christian morality go hand-in-hand and exist *only* when they are together. We talk of having the courage of our convictions and the ability to act on those convictions, but we forget where those convictions originate.

Parents teach morality to children. There is no neutrality when it comes to raising moral children. How many times have we heard the response, "We don't want to prejudice our children about God, so we will let them decide about church when they are grown up"? How many parents have lulled themselves into a false sense of security about teaching morality to children only to find that when their children are grown, they believe exactly what their parents believe—often next to nothing! And how many parents have groaned at the realization that their attempts to be neutral on moral issues have built such a weakness into their young people that they have virtually no resistance to the invitations of the world to behave immorally?

Morality is having the power to say "no!"

How Morality is Learned

Morality must be taught. There must be effort expended by

179

parents and directed at their children. While the Bible teaches that every person must ultimately answer for his own behavior (Romans 14:10-12), parents have an unusual responsibility to answer to God for how they taught biblical morality to *His* children.

Parents control moral learning in most family situations. Here are some of the parental behaviors that have shown to make a difference.

Moral maturity and moral discernment are encouraged by mothers who are non-threatening to their children. I am not talking about weak, non-disciplining mothers, but rather mothers who do not *threaten* their children into good behavior. When the primary parent in the lives of young children (usually the mother) relies on threats and overt power to get children to behave, she unwittingly deprives them of opportunities to think about right and wrong. Mothers who attempt to explain things to their young children and talk them into doing right will get better results in the long run. A disappointed mother is more effective in instilling personal responsibility in children than is a punitive mother.

Our focus on Mom in this discussion is because mother is the primary caregiver in the early years, and it is during these years that a moral sense is acquired. Morality is strengthened and buttressed by later experiences that often involve Dad, but the early years belong to Mom.

Another point is that when mother uses the teaching method known as "induction," she gets better results. Induction simply means that when issues of morality come up at home, perhaps a discussion of whether or not it is okay to keep a toy found on the sidewalk or look for its owner, mothers who involve their children in the discussion and in the decision do a better job of teaching moral principles. Induction means the child participates in moral decisions and is thus encouraged to take responsibility for them at an early age. Being responsible is often what we mean when we talk of having morality, whether in children, teenagers, or adults.

Mothers who attempt to control the behavior of their

children by threatening them with the loss of love can expect to have problems with their children. We know that "love-withdrawal" discourages moral development. Yes, it makes the child more dependent on Mom and may produce obedience, but obedience alone is not morality. A child or teenager may be well-behaved and moral but for the wrong reasons. Eventally Mom or Dad will not be around anymore, and the motivation for doing right may vanish. Parents should not threaten their children with the loss of love for misbehavior. God does not treat us that way, and we should not treat our children in any way that does not model God.

We also find that as long as discipline is firm and consistent, the method of disciplining makes little difference. The key is the message conveyed to children by discipline rather than by the method chosen to administer that discipline. It also seems that mother can be as effective a disciplinarian as father. Granted, most Christians expect Dad to do the dirty work if he is home, but there is no reason Mom can't step in and administer the discipline when Dad's gone.

It is the *act* of discipline that matters, not the method or the person.

We know that when postive emotions are expressed in the home, moral development is encouraged. Positive emotions are hugs, kisses, compliments, pats on the back, and smiles to name just a few. Note that these positive emotions are supposed to occur both between parents and children *and* between the parents themselves. Children need to see positive emotions expressed between Mom and Dad because this simple act shows the kids that they are secure. Don't forget, about half of the kids in your child's class at school have gone through a divorce. When children don't have to worry about their parents, then they have the freedom to internalize the moral lessons they are learning.

Children do not learn well under stress. If the family is healthy and in good shape, children worry less and learn better, including moral lessons.

Moral Development

For several years I had the privilege of helping supervise children's church at our home church in Michigan. In the course of that undertaking, I shared in many special programs aimed at evangelizing elementary-aged children. Most were excellent programs that took the Bible and the children's level of understanding into consideration.

But one Sunday I faced a problem in children's church. A movie was scheduled to be shown to the kids that day as part of the service. A movie that was, we were told, very evangelistic and spiritually productive.

The title of the movie is not important now, but the subject of it was hell. I could not believe what I was seeing. Here were almost 200 children, from first grade to sixth grade, watching a film about hell that included fire, screams, and a devil-like personage. It was a film that was terrifying to *me* and the other adults in children's church, never mind the children.

I grabbed our two and left. There was no way I going to expose them to a "children's" movie that had as its sole aim scaring children into some kind of pseudo-decision for the Lord.

What a travesty!

Whoever made that movie probably had good intentions but was not educated enough to realize that children have different levels of moral understanding, and evangelistic messages must *always* be tailored to the specific age-group involved. When speaking to children between five and 12, for example, we are speaking to at least three different levels of understanding about moral issues. It can be virtually assured that most of the children in a group like that will be bored or confused by the presentation. We need to be as careful presenting our message to groups of children as we are when we structure our Sunday School classes along age lines. To fail to take this into account guarantees the failure of the message.

Three Levels of Moral Development

There seems to be general agreement that moral development occurs in three stages or levels. The major theorist of this idea is Laurence Kohlberg, the well-known expert on the development of morality in children. [1] He divided moral development into levels he called the preconventional, conventional, and postconventional.

The *preconventional level* of moral development is believed to take place between birth and the beginning of school. This level or stage is characterized by a simple punishment and reward attitude. Very small children seem to understand right and wrong based solely on what happens following the behavior. Good behavior is that which produces a reward of some kind while bad behavior gets spanked, scolded, or stood in the corner. There seems to be no understanding yet of *why* the behavior is right or wrong, just that it is.

At this level, obedience and good behavior are based on the need to receive rewards from important adults like Mom and Dad. Mom's smile or Dad's hug encourage children to repeat a behavior. Mom's frown or Dad's slap tell the child he had better *not* repeat the behavior.

The second level of moral development covers the years between the ages of five and 12, roughly elementary school age. Kohlberg calls this period the *conventional stage* because of the elementary school child's absorption with rules and regulations. Children at this age are legalistic in the extreme and base their ideas of good and bad behavior on the rules they know. Being a good or bad child depends on whether or not they meet the expectations of important adults like parents and teachers. It is at this age that some children come to believe that some rules are made to be broken.

During the conventional period of moral development, children need to know their limitations in order to feel secure and protected. The absence of rules or the existence of rules that are stated too generally create stress for children and often result in rebellious misbehavior that seems to have no direct cause. Elementary school aged children gain security and self-confidence when they know exactly what is expected of them. When teaching this age group, we need to make sure they know precisely what we are talking about and why they should accept what we are telling them as truth.

I recall the day in the summer of 1981 our family moved to Lynchburg, our present home in central Virginia. Of our three children, only ten-year-old Jennifer was with us, the older two were coming later because of commitments in South Carolina.

While Linda and I were busy working with the moving men, trying to get things settled, some neighborhood girls came down and asked Jennifer to play. They proceeded to set up the sprinkler on the front lawn and seemed to be arranging a kind of water tag game. What struck me was that for the first hour or so they seemed to be doing more talking than playing. On listening more carefully, I discovered that was exactly what they were doing. And what they were talking and arguing about were the rules of the game they wanted to play. They had to have rules, or they couldn't play! When they finally got the game going, the slightest violation sent things into chaos.

Elementary school-aged children are legalistic in the extreme! Rules are absolutely essential to reduce ambiguities and provide structure for an immature mind. Moral questions are settled on the basis of rules for this age group, a fact parents and teachers need to have emphasized from time to time. Sunday School lessons need to be carefully tailored to provide structure and security while stimulating their spiritual curiosity.

Then, as expected, elementary aged children become middle school and high school young people, slowly moving into the adult realm of moral reasoning. Oddly, it is this movement to adult thought that creates the most stress for parents even though the changes are what they have been looking for all along.

The problem for Christian parents of teenagers is that often their new moral understanding is perceived as rebellion. Too frequently our fear of *any* kind of independent thought in our young people creates a knee-jerk reaction to even the most innocent of questions.

"Why do we go to church on Wednesday night?" Asked by a ninth grader, this question frightens parents. It seems to signal that they are beginning to lose the battle with the world when, in reality, the asking of the question is a very positive sign in Christian kids. The kids we are losing to the world are not asking any questions; they have already made up their minds. So when new ideas and questions pop up, they must be dealt with maturely. Calm, rational responses will meet a teenager's needs in most Christian families whereas over-reaction or legalistic rebuttal will convince him that his parents don't really know *why* church is the place to be on Wednesday night.

What is it that leads some children to become moral leaders early in life?

Why do some of our young people grow to spiritual maturity so much earlier than others, and have the courage and conviction to act on what they believe to be right?

As I stated at the beginning of this chapter, moral maturity must spring from something; it is never created in a vacuum. While recognizing that God rules and is sovereign in the affairs of men, He has nevertheless given parents a role to play in moral development.

Developing Spirit Led Independence in Young People

God can overrule the effects of bad parenting. He has the power to take a child from a bad family and provide the opportunities for moral maturity should the young person choose to act on those opportunities. However, we see in our churches the results of a lost testimony by a Christian parent. We see bitterness and anger that may take years, even generations to wipe away. And, we are told that the sins of the fathers can be passed on to following generations (Exodus 20:5). But we know that parents have the God-given power to be influential in the lives of our children for *good* if we are careful about our lives.

After God, parents have the most important role to play in developing moral maturity and Spirit-led independence in young people.

Parents who take it upon themselves to explain things to their children and teenagers encourage moral maturity and independence. Having the freedom to ask questions in an open and non-threatening atmosphere gives young people the feeling that Mom and Dad are secure in their beliefs and convictions. Such comfortable, non-structured conversation stimulates the mind of a young person. Stimulation is entertainment for the brain. Parents who provide interesting *and* safe things for their kids to think about build a natural immunity to the lure of sinful thoughts.

We can't expect perfection for our children and teenagers. Their imagination and curiosity will almost surely lead them to look at that pornographic picture or try that cigarette or bottle of beer. The thing that distinguishes a Christian young person who just *tries* from one who continues to *use* is often the family attitude in which he or she was raised. Parents want to stay away from the extremes of permissiveness and authoritarianism. Both will push Christian young people into continuing the negative behaviors mentioned and many more. The pressure comes from different directions and for different reasons, but the result is the same.

It is the young person from *reasonable* Christian families, those who talk about smoking, drinking, and sex without scaring their children, who tend to be successful in developing moral maturity. The *permissive* Christian parent often implies permission to practice sinful behavior. These moms and dads neutralize sin so that it is no longer negative. The super-strict, *authoritarian* parent gives the sinful behavior a magical quality that often increases the young person's sense of temptation to try it.

It is a middle-of-the-road approach that is needed, one that can avoid the dangers of the deep ditches of extremity on either side.

Parenting style makes a difference in the development of moral maturity. Research has shown that over-protective parents actually slow down a young person's move to moral maturity, primarily because of the hidden message contained in "smother" love. When parents over-protect and try to raise children in a "hot house" environment free of contamination from the outside, what develops is a child or teenager who looks good on the outside but is weak and vulnerable on the inside. The over-protected child has simply not built up any immunities to the negative forces outside the family. As soon as they leave the home, they become quickly and, sometimes, fatally infected.

Over-protective parents appear to be exercising parent power as they raise their children when, in reality, they have surrendered their power to the fear they feel. Choosing to isolate rather than innoculate, they make their children vulnerable. Over-protective parents love their children but do not trust God or the Holy Spirit to protect. Over-protective parents are trying to do God's work for Him.

Another parent behavior that makes a difference in developing moral maturity and Spirit-led independence in young people is the parent's attitude about parenting itself. When parents are confident in their God-given responsibility to raise children and teenagers, that feeling of "I can do it" is sensed by youngsters and will be imitated. This is especially powerful when Mother feels good about herself as a parent because her sense of confidence is picked up by very young children and strengthens their sense of security.

Self-confident Christian parents who are able to trust the Holy Spirit to lead them in making the right decisions for children model God-centered confident living for their children.

Discipline is an important issue as well when considering moral maturity in young people. We know with certainty that firm control is essential in developing well-behaved and morally sensitive children as long as the control is not so firm that it restricts opportunities to learn. Once again, discipline is another building block in a child's security sanctuary. As long as the sanctuary does not become a prison that separates the child from opportunities to learn, moral maturity is encouraged.

In this regard, let's think about limits.

Limits are essential in every aspect of life. We face limitations on our behavior at every turn, from the traffic signals to the time clock and production reports at work. We all face time limitations, and we know generally what must be accomplished in the time allowed. Limits provide safety and structure for living. They are indispensable.

Children and adolescents must learn to deal with limits. They will face them with increasing frequency later in life. Permissive parents are not doing their children a favor when they fail to teach living within limits. Authoritarian parents are not being good to their children when they place such restrictive limits on their children that opportunities to learn are allowed to bypass them. Young people feel secure when reasonable limits are enforced and learn valuable lessons that should make living easier and more productive.

Limits are positive in the life of a Christian!

Since we are discussing limitations and discipline, we need to say something about rewarding children for good behavior.

In studying this subject, we find that excessive reliance on rewards to get children to obey and behave properly actually discourages moral maturity. When children are bribed to obey, they come to expect a reward for normal good behavior. The pay-off becomes *the reason* for their good behavior, and as soon as a reward is not offered, the good behavior may vanish.

The question, then, is why children and adolescents obey their parents and behave themselves. What is their motivation for doing right?

Jamie, The Business Boy

Ed and Joann Smithson were referred to me by their pastor. Their nine-year-old son Jamie was slowly becoming a behavior problem, and Ed and Joann were running out of remedies.

As we talked the first time, I discovered that Jamie's parents were college educated people and were each successful in separate occupations. The family was reasonably well-off due to two above average incomes, and Jamie was their only child.

Ed and Joann revealed that they had been taught the value of behavior modification techniques while in college during the seventies and had been trying to apply some of the principles to their parenting practices. Early on they had taught their son that good behavior results in rewards and bad

188

behavior results in punishment or loss of reward, depending on the seriousness of the bad behavior. Jamie had learned to expect a reward for obedience.

But as Jamie got older, he seemed to realize that he could bargain with his parents. If he did not think the reward was worth his effort, he would not obey. He was smart enough to know where the line was and could avoid a spanking while continuing to nag and whine until his mom or dad would give in.

Jamie had started a business with his parents as customers. What he had to sell was obedience and good behavior, and the selling price was whatever the market would bear.

In applying the principles of modern behaviorism to child-rearing, Ed and Joann Smithson had created a parent's nightmare. They had never allowed Jamie to experience guilt for his wrongdoing because he could always "buy" his way out of trouble by promising to behave properly. When Mom and Dad were not around and no reward was possible, there was no still small voice called conscience telling Jamie to behave.

We had some serious restructuring to do with the Smithson family, but Jamie was young enough that we could be optimistic. The most important thing Ed and Joann needed to do was gradually phase out the reward structure so that Jamie would be encouraged to do right for no apparent reason.

The mindset in children *should* go something like this:

I am sitting here wanting a cookie from the cookie jar right over there on the kitchen counter. I have been scolded and even spanked for taking a cookie without permission just before dinner, but lately I have gotten away with it a few times. I guess Mom didn't notice.

But it was sure funny that I felt bad about eating the cookie when I didn't get caught. I didn't feel bad when I did get caught because I got hollered at or spanked and that seemed to satisfy everybody.

So why am I not making a grab for a cookie now?

I want one!

Mom's not here right now!

Why am I just sitting here?
I guess I don't want to risk making myself *feel bad by doing what I know is wrong. I guess I can wait!*

Jamie's parents need to let their son experience the guilt of doing wrong and the satisfacton that comes from doing right, even when there is no external reward. Ed and Joann need to be sure they compliment Jamie for being a good boy and discipline him when he behaves badly, but conscience comes from within. Rewards and punishments that occur too frequently discourage moral development.

Moral maturity and Spirit led independence are built into children; they do not happen on their own or by accident. Our behavior as parents has more to do with the process than any other single thing. If we can remind ourselves that we are our children's role models and behave accordingly, good results can be expected.

Why Good Kids Choose Negative Friends

Let's focus on teenagers for awhile, now. One of the most common problems facing Christian parents raising adolescents has to do with their friends. While some of this ground was covered in an earlier chapter, the issue often takes on moral overtones and needs to be addressed.

Christian teenagers are like all other teens except they are Christians. It may sound like a flip statement but the point is that we need to see our young people as just that—young people with all the same temptations and questions as any others. So as we look at this question, we need to remember that because of the age-bound immaturity in most young people, Christian or not, the issue of choosing friends will come up.

Christian teens sometimes choose marginal or bad friends because they are exciting. There is a natural tendency in all teenagers to experiment which often leads them to go beyond their boundaries even if only for a little while. The need to experiment will be less dangerous in most Christian teens because of the limitations usually already in place. But the need is still there.

Another reason Christian adolescents choose marginal or bad friends relates to identity development. The natural curiosity of adolescence leads to attempts at making friends with kids who are known to be unacceptable to parents. It is not so much rebellion as information-gathering, learning about other lifestyles and other ways of doing things.

We also need to remember that teenagers are almost helpless when it comes to turning down an offer of friendship. Adolescents cannot have too many friends, and if a few marginal friends slip in, what's the problem? Often the young person senses that the purpose is information and excitement rather than lifestyle change. Parents need to be sensitive to their young person. Some teens are so lonely or insecure, that they will seek the company of anyone who will accept them. They willingly accept the lifestyle change necessary for that acceptance and a downward spiral begins.

Christian parents have more influence on their growing children than any force the world can muster. We need to remind ourselves of the power God has placed within us and know that He is in charge of the lives He has loaned us to raise.

The Big Question

Christian parents face many heartrending questions about raising children in the nurture and admonition of the Lord, but surely the most basic has to do with the role parents play in their children accepting the Lord as their personal Saviour. Many of us have been quick to "amen" a preacher who says "God has no grandchildren." Quick, that is, until we stop to think what it is we are saying amen about.

God has no grandchildren!

Every human being with the capacity to understand the gospel message must choose to accept or reject Christ for himself or herself. There are no shortcuts.

But what about our children? Are parents helpless in determining the salvation of their children? Is there nothing we can do to encourage the right decision? What is the role of parents in the decision of a young person to accept or reject Christ?

191

Look with me at some of the issues surrounding this very important question.

Probably the most commonly cited passage on this subject is found in the book of Proverbs.

Train up a child in the way he should go: and when he is old, he will not depart from it.   Proverbs 22:6

Several well-known pastors and evangelists have told me over the years that this passage is one of the most poorly understood in all the Bible. Many or most take this verse to mean an absolute guarantee that if parents "train up" a child correctly "in the way he should go," later on in adulthood "he will not depart from it."

However, my research has led me to believe that this verse has very little to do with what we would call parenting and much to do with education. The verse, according to my commentaries and the Bible scholars I have asked, states a simple practical message encouraging parents to identify a child's aptitude and abilities and to train that child in an appropriate occupation. And there is a deeper spiritual message to emphasize godly behavior and personal responsibility—a conscience.

God's sovereignty always supersedes man's understanding.

Proverbs 22:6 is not a guarantee that certain parent behaviors will assure the salvation of a child. God really does not have any grandchildren. Our individual, personal responsibility to accept Christ is a paramount doctrine of Scripture. It is never excused or abrogated.

Let me emphasize the point this way. Stay with me. I have a point to make that relates to Christian parents.

We are presently living in the Church Age, a time most Bible scholars believe immediately precedes the rapture of the Church, the resurrection of the saints, and the beginning of the tribulation period lasting seven years. At the time of the rapture, all believers will be "taken away upward" to meet the Lord in the air (I Thessalonians 4:13-18).

During the tribulation, Satan reigns. The mark of the beast is required and great persecution is commonplace.

At the conclusion of the tribulation, judgment occurs. Jesus returns with the saints to rule the earth in perfection for 1,000 years known as the millenium.

At the end of the seven year period of the tribulation, all unbelievers are judged and removed. Jesus Christ is on earth in person. All sin is immediately dealt with, and Satan is bound, totally helpless for 1,000 years.

Almost complete perfection on earth. We have to settle for near perfection because we are told that Jesus will rule with a "rod of iron" that would be unnecessary if there were no sin (Revelation 2:27).

Then, at the end of the 1,000 years, Satan is released from his prison in anticipation of the end-times war between good and evil. He will go about the earth gathering all the unsaved to join him in battle.

And when the thousand years are expired, Satan shall be loosed out of his prison, And shall go out to deceive the nations which are in the four quarters of the earth, Gog and Magog, to gather them together to battle: the number of whom is as the sand of the sea. Revelation 20:7-8

The question is this: If, at the beginning of the millenium, *all* the unsaved are removed from the earth for judgment, where did the millions and millions of unsaved people in Revelation 20:8 come from?

This is not a trick question, but it does go to the heart of the concern we have as Christian parents.

The obvious answer is that resurrected and raptured saints will not reproduce during the millenium. Those who were saved during the seven-year tribulation and entered the millenium in their physical bodies *will* marry and bear children during this time. They are the grandchildren, great-grandchildren, *et cetera,* of those who were saved during the tribulation and who survived Satan's persecution to enter the millenium.

The point is this. If, during 1,000 years of near-perfection, with Jesus living among us and known to all—with sin being judged immediately and nothing overlooked—if during this time some will choose to reject Jesus in spite of all the encouragements to become a Christian—how, then, can we living today be surprised when some of our children choose to reject Christ?

Please note this as a message of comfort.

Parents do *not* have total control of the eternal decisions of their children. To pretend that Proverbs 22:6 means that if parents perform well, their children *will* become Christians is to remove the need for Calvary and nullify the work of the Holy Spirit.

We parents do *not* have the final say in the spiritual decisions of our children. We are more influential in their lives than any others on this earth, but we do not control the eternal destiny of the children God gave us to raise for Him. Salvation is never forced on anyone, children or adults. We are not bad parents if one or more of our children reject Christ.

Is God a bad parent because 100% of His children rebelled and sinned? Of course not. God created free will so He could love us as more than mere puppets with no will of our own. God created free will so we could *choose* to love Him.

The message of Proverbs 22:6 is one of good, careful parenting, not of eternal responsibility for the spiritual decisions of another human being. The message of Revelation 20:7-8 reminds us that it is God who is in charge.

A Final Word on Morality

The fact that parents do not have the final word on the spiritual decisions of their children in no way lessens our responsibility to be good parents. Rather than attempting to open the door to heaven for our children, we should, instead, concentrate on removing roadblocks and straightening out detours. The key to heaven is kept in God's hand, but parents can point out the door for their children (Revelation 3:20). Parents can, by life, word, and use of Scripture, introduce their child to Christ and that should be their heart's desire and goal. The decision, however, is still personal.

The issue that faces me most frequently in the counseling office is that of parents who are still struggling with their responsibility for the immoral and sinful behavior of a teenage or adult offspring.

The question I am asked more than any other is, "What did we do wrong?" "What did we miss doing or do too much that caused our son or daughter to turn away from Jesus and reject what he/she has been taught?"

My answer is to go through a discussion of Proverbs and chapters of the book of Revelation to help them see the limits God has placed on our responsibility with our children. A careful examination of the issue of moral development and parental responsibility will reveal parents as the *second* most influential person in their moral development. The first, of course, is God Himself. Our limitations as human parents in no way reduces our responsibility to model the best image of God we can for our young children. The fact that we cannot do everything does not mean we should not do *anything!*

Our role is to model God in front of our children. We are to live moral lives so that our children will grow to belive that morality is normal rather than abnormal. What we do for our children, we do in love, conscious of the heavy responsibility God has placed in our hands and mindful that He asks no more of us than His grace will enable us to bear.

It is in God's plan for moral parents to produce moral children. But this is not in perfect predictive terms. If there were a guarantee that good parenting would produce good, moral children, the work of the Holy Spirit would be in vain. Sometimes moral parents produce immoral young people, a fact that is guaranteed by the doctrine of free will. The fact that not everyone who hears the gospel will accept its offer of salvation in no way reduces our responsibility to proclaim that gospel. The fact that some of our children will reject Christ in no way diminishes our need to do everything we can to present the offer in the best way we know.

FOOTNOTES:
[1] Kohlberg, L., *Moral Development and Behavior* 1976, Holt, Rinehart & Winston, NY, NY.

11
STRENGTHENING YOUR FAMILY TREE

*There are only two
lasting bequests
we can give
our children—
one is roots
the other, wings.*
Anonymous

The Power to Grow

The family is supposed to be a fertile seedbed in which children can flourish and grow until strong enough to branch out on their own. God intends parents to provide all that is needed within the broad boundaries of nurture and admonition. As the anonymous poet said, roots and wings are the most important legacies for our children.

Nurture *and* admonition.

Love *and* power.

Neither can function without the other. A family that loves its children but lacks the will or strength to discipline and instruct corrupts the young child's concept of God. Permissive parents present an image of God as one who loves but does not care enough to help, nurtures but does not admonish. Authoritarian parents corrupt a young child's image of God even more by showing them a God who controls but does not love.

Permissive parents provide a seedbed that is rich and fertile but open to the elements. It is a ground where seeds sprout easily but are lost quickly to wind and cold, disease and lack of tending. It is a place of growth that is friendly and warm in the beginning but lacks those strong enough to build a hedge around the young plants so they may be protected. Permissive parents love but lack power. Permissive parents accept only partial responsibility as parents, choosing to assign the rest to circumstances and the elements of this world.

Authoritarian parents have power but lack love. Authoritarian parents are capable of loving but fear the results of dispersing it too easily to the children. Strong parents are often afraid of losing their power to the "softness" of love.

Authoritarian parents build a strong seedbed for children to grow. There are strong hedges to protect from invaders and the elements and many to care for the young, but the seedbed itself is weak and infertile, lacking in warmth and nurturing. Authoritarian parents develop good-looking seedbeds to show to their friends and other parents, but along the way too many of the young wither and die from lack of care or are drawn off and put down roots in a more tempting environment. There are many casualties in authoritarian families.

The biblical model of Christian parenting is the middle ground between permissive and authoritarian, a more reasonable and biblical concept within which children can grow to become honoring to both God and parents. The authoritative (not authoritarian) seedbed is characterized by a well-nourished foundation in which to begin life, protected from the elements by a strong hedge of limited height so that children can see beyond it as they grow.

Innoculated without being isolated, children in authoritative families develop immunities to the diseases and temptations of the world by controlled exposure to the elements. Authoritative parents grow good young children but understand that there may be a time of temporary loss when they grow tall enough to see beyond the family hedge. Such parents model God's patience and confidence by knowing and acting as if their children will turn out well, even in spite of temporary setbacks.

Authoritative parents are content to wait until children are fully grown before making judgments about the relative "goodness" of each, and even then are able to show godly optimism because their trust is not in themselves, but in God.

197

Authoritative parents enjoy being parents!

The Power to be Independent

Strong roots give children the power to withstand the winds of temptation and sin. Conservative Christian parents sometimes have difficulty distinguishing independence from rebellion in their children, something that has had disastrous consequences in many families.

Having the power to say "no" was discussed earlier. I want to emphasize here that saying *no* to the world is what we should want in our young people. But in order to see that power manifested in children and teenagers, parents must accept some trial-and-error learning along the way. We cannot have such an absolute standard of behavior for young people that there is no chance of making a mistake. Learning grows from error, and if errors are not allowed, learning will not occur either.

Learning to say no to the world requires parents who can tolerate an occasional yes answer that creates problems. It is not that parents need to tolerate sin, but, rather, to be able to be understanding of errors in judgment.

Our oldest daughter wanted to date a boy we believed unsuitable. We debated and argued and were strongly tempted to put down the parental foot and pronounce an absolute "no." But reason prevailed, and we allowed the date to take place in our home (the first time at least) so that circumstances could be controlled if we were right about this fellow.

There seemed to be no problem and a few more dates took place. Then we did not see or hear any more of this young man. As curiosity got the better of us, we asked Laurie what became of him.

"Oh, we just don't have very much in common," was her reply.

We resisted the opportunity to say, "We told you so," and opted for a question and answer period instead. We found that Laurie had much better judgment than we had given her credit for and all she needed was the independence (controlled, though it was) to make up her own mind. Laurie,

198

our first teenager, found the power to decide that a boy who wanted to see her was not suitable, and he was dropped.

Power is independence, and independence is power.

What we learned from this early skirmish with adolescence served us well in the years that followed. Although we often found ourselves walking through the valley of the shadow of adolescence, we knew God had already given us the power to raise our children the way He wished.

Reciprocal Gifts

How often have you heard someone proclaim children to be gifts from the hand of God?

And how many times have you been tempted to say, "Some gift!"

There is a natural tendency in us both to accept and sometimes resent the idea of our children being gifts to us. Even in the face of such passages as Psalm 127:3: *Lo, children are an heritage of the Lord: and the fruit of the womb is his reward.*

Consider this idea for a moment.

Consider the possibility that *parents* are the primary and most important gifts in the family. Wonder with me if it doesn't make more sense to see ourselves as being given by God to the children who need *us* rather than vice versa.

We know that the "giving" priority in the Bible is always parents to children. We know as well that in everyday family life, when the order of giving becomes reversed so that children become the emotional providers for parents, the family is always in trouble. When we find cases of child abuse and sexual abuse in a family, it always seems to be that the giving-getting order has been reversed.

In child abuse, Mom or Dad depends too much on a child for emotional support and love. Thus, when the inevitable misbehavior occurs, it is seen not as simple misbehavior, but as rejection and lack of love.

In cases of sexual abuse in families, somehow the parental giving of love and emotional support to the children has reversed so that the children become providers of these things

199

to a parent. When children become providers, the family is breaking down.

Parents give to children. Children are blessings to us and responsibilities at the same time.

Parents are blessings to children but are not supposed to be burdens to them, at least not in their childhood.

Now, if you were God, how would you structure things?

When Linda and I had our first child, we had been on this earth a combined total of 43 years. God had saved us, educated us, given each of us a wealth of experiences, and provided each of us with a family as we grew up.

When we received Laurie that November day, three weeks before President Kennedy was killed, she had no ability to meet our needs at all. In fact, she was totally dependent on us for her very survival.

Was Laurie a "gift" to us or were we gifts to her?

She was and continues to be a blessing to us, but she has been much more of a burden to us than we to her, as it should be.

I would suggest that we have been looking at our roles as parents in the wrong light. God has prepared each parent to meet the special needs of his children. God has not prepared the child to meet the needs of parents.

Who, then, is the gift?

Imagine God planning to send a newborn baby into an expectant family. And let's suppose that this particular baby will be one of the ten percent who develop a learning disability. Would it not be reasonable that God would give that child to a set of parents He knows can raise him well? I wonder sometimes if we overdo it when we give heavy compliments to parents who have never had trouble with their children and have faced no major difficulties.

Perhaps it is good parenting that produced such good results.

Or, perhaps God gave that set of parents children He knew would present no major problems because He knew the limitations of the parents.

I hope this doesn't sound blasphemous to imagine what

might be in the mind of God on the subject of parenting. I just think we have been putting ourselves down as Christian parents for far too long.

I believe *we* are gifts to our children!

Power Parenting is a Choice

There will be no excuses when we face God. Those of us who are Christians probably feel pretty good compared to unbelievers, but I wonder if we sometimes miss the point.

During the years we are assigned to be parents, God surely expects us to be as influential for good with our children as possible. How will we answer the question about why we did not do more to raise His children in the nurture and admonition we were told about? How will we explain our permissiveness in letting our young people attend rock concerts we *knew* were wrong but felt pressured to okay? How will we explain our dogmatic legalism in raising our children to believe that this or that Bible believing group were not at the same level of "good" Christianity as our little group?

Will we have the courage to say to Jesus that we made a choice down there on earth, and, at the time, it seemed the right thing to do?

I wonder!

Will we have the intestinal fortitude to say that in giving permission to see a movie or to listen to a certain kind of music, we were following the still small voice of the Holy Spirit?

Or will we say the Devil made us do it?

I wonder what I will say!

I know that I chose to have the amount of Bible knowledge I have at this moment. If I wanted more, I would have turned off that hockey game last night and read my Bible some more. I know I chose to watch the hockey game!

When our children were little, Linda and I chose to have family devotions, attend church regularly, tithe, visit, work in the nursery, usher, and teach Sunday School. I am happy about those choices, and we have continued these aspects of ministry all these years.

We chose to discipline our children along the lines we believed the Bible teaches. This has not changed over time. We chose to let our teenagers date at a certain age, get a driver's license at 16, and even gave our consent for a marriage.

We chose to do all these things; none of them were forced upon us.

And as independent human beings we chose exactly what we wanted our three children to be able to do when the time comes for *them* to choose. The freedom to choose is one of God's greatest gifts to mankind, and it affects every aspect of living, from who will change the diaper on the new baby to whether to continue life support for a dying spouse.

Choice! What a gift! What a responsibility!

We Are Not Alone

We had a crisis in our family several years ago. I'm telling this story now in the last part of the book because it has taken me this long to work up the courage to share this with you. Though it turned out well, the crisis took over a year to resolve itself, and in some ways it is still with me.

The details are not important anymore, but for two days and a night, Linda and I did not know where one of our children was. We were living in South Carolina at the time, and when we received a call from our child's employer asking why our child had not shown up for work that Saturday, we were panic stricken.

One of our children, at age 16, had left home.

We were parents of a runaway!

We did not know if our teenager was dead or alive for two days and a night. We did not sleep at all that Saturday night. We called everyone we could think of who might know our child's whereabouts without success.

I drove to every motel in our city that Saturday night, trying to discover if anyone had seen our 16-year-old.

I sat in the car and cried. For the first time in my adult life, I cried.

I felt so alone. I know Linda did, too, but our pain was so

great that it was difficult to console one another.

All day Saturday, all through that night, and all day Sunday we waited, and cried and hoped until we got a phone call at 6:30 asking for a meeting to talk about a problem we honestly did not know existed.

Looking back on that crisis in the Miller family, I can see why it is so difficult to help people in crisis.

Yes, everything *eventually* settled down and some good lessons were learned by all the family members. But we felt so alone then. We felt abandoned by the God we had served and continue to serve.

We felt abandoned, but now we know that we were *not* alone in that crisis. Our child was protected in some potentially dangerous situations that weekend, and Linda and I did not crack under the strain of not knowing. God knew we could bear what was occurring in our family.

God gave us the *power* to deal with the situation, and we did.

We are not alone, even in the dark days of parenting.

Christian parents are never alone, and I believe we receive special strength for special circumstances like dealing with a rebellious teenager. We are not alone, because we have the Holy Spirit to comfort and guide us as we walk through the valley of the shadow of difficult children. That crisis was the worst we had faced up to that point, but we have faced even more serious situations since. But God was and is able to meet our needs.

Faithful is he that calleth you (parents), *who will also do it.* I Thessalonians 5:24

Future Thoughts

Experience teaches some heavy lessons about parenting, and it is on this note that I conclude.

If there is any reasonable way to predict what Christian parents will face in the days ahead, it must be based on an accurate understanding of the dichotomy we face in our families. We see the world moving farther and farther away from traditional Judeo-Christian values of family, God, and nation. Our children will grow up into a world far different than what we see before us now.

Yes, I know it may sound corny and old-fashioned, but the reality is that the world is changing so fast that it boggles the minds of even the experts. Future shock is a term coined by one writer to explain the degree of adjustment required to deal with an increasingly complex and challenging world. And it is real.

I would not volunteer to start my life over again if I had to begin living now. I cannot imagine the obstacles our children and grandchildren will have to overcome to maintain their testimony for Jesus Christ.

But note this as you consider these points. God is still able to meet the needs of His children living in the world He created. We are expected to do the best job we can in raising our children and equipping them with the necessary armor to fend off and attack the evils of the world.

Our job is in preparation. Our task as Christian parents is to fight the good fight *at home* in the sense of keeping the world away from our children until they are well-trained and strong enough to do battle and win. Our job is to remove roadblocks to spiritual living, to warn of potential detours and rabbit trails that sap energy, and to point the way to the One who holds not only the map but the final outcome of the battle.

We are training Christian soldiers, whether we like it or not. Expect a battle, and you will be ready when it arrives. Expect the world to try to infiltrate your home and family with diversions and detours.

Then, be prepared to say with Joshua of old, "as for me and my house, we *will* serve the Lord."

About the Author

Dr. David R. Miller is a professor of psychology at Liberty University in Lynchburg, Virginia. He and his wife Linda were both saved in 1961. They have three children and are committed to the family unit under God.

Dr. Miller believes strongly in the need for powerful Christian parenting. He has taught in the Detroit school system and counseled hundreds of parents and children, seeing the results of power loss over and over again. His work as a counselor has also shown him the need to fortify the Christian family, to strengthen our godly parenting heritage and make it resistant to the world's secularization.

Dr. Miller is the author of over three dozen articles on family issues and counseling. *Parent Power—Godly Influence in an Age of Weakness* is his first book.